# RUMKOWSKI

## and the Orphans of Lodz

# RUMKOWSKI

## and the Orphans of Lodz

## Lucille Eichengreen

with Rebecca Camhi Fromer

MERCURY HOUSE—SAN FRANCISCO

Published in the United States by Mercury House, San Francisco, California,
a nonprofit publishing company devoted to the free exchange of ideas and guided
by a dedication to literary values. Mercury House and colophon
are registered trademarks of Mercury House, Incorporated.
Visit us at www.wenet.net/~mercury.

*United States Constitution, First Amendment:*
Congress shall make no law respecting an establishment of religion, or
prohibiting the free exercise thereof; or abridging the freedom of speech, or of the
press; or the right of the people peaceably to assemble, and to petition
the Government for a redress of grievances.

Cover photograph: *"Rumkowski besucht eine offentliche Kuche,"* Lodz Ghetto,
photographer unknown. Jüdisches Museum, Frankfurt.

*Photo credits:* Title page photo © Mendel Grossman, from *The Chronicle of the Lodz
Ghetto, 1941–1944,* edited by Lucjan Dobroszycki (Yale University Press, 1984). Photos
on pp. 2, 28, 91, 98 courtesy of Yad Vashem: The Holocaust Martyrs' and Heroes'
Remembrance Authority, PO Box 3477, Jerusalem 91034. Photos on pp. 8, 13, 23, 38,
50, 56, 86 courtesy of Jüdisches Museum, Untermainkai 14/15, 60311 Frankfurt a.M.,
Germany. Photos on pp. 49, 74, 93 courtesy of Zydowski Instytut Historyczny, ul.
Tlomackie 3/5, 00-090 Warszawa, Poland. Illustration on p. 112 courtesy of Yivo
Institute for Jewish Research, 15 West 16th Street, New York, NY 10019.

Designed and typeset by Kirsten Janene-Nelson.
Additional editorial and production work by Jeremy Bigalke, Justin Edgar,
Tamara Straus, and Amy Widestrom.

This book is made possible in part by generous support from the
Richard & Rhoda Goldman Fund.

Printed on acid-free 55" Miami Book Cream paper and manufactured by
Hignell Book Printing, Ltd., Winnipeg, Manitoba, Canada.

*Library of Congress Cataloging-in-Publication Data:*
Eichengreen, Lucille, 1925–
    Rumkowski and the orphans of Lodz / Lucille Eichengreen with Rebecca Camhi
Fromer.
    p.   cm.
    ISBN 1-56279-115-x (trade pbk.)
    1. Eichengreen, Lucille, 1925–   . 2. Jews—Germany—Hamburg Biography.
3. Holocaust, Jewish (1939–1945)—Poland—Lodz Personal narratives. 4. Jewish
children in the Holocaust—Poland—Lodz Biography. 5. Rumkowski, Mordecai
Hayim. 6. Hamburg (Germany) Biography. 7. Lodz (Poland) Biography.
I. Fromer, Rebecca. II. Title.
DS135.G5E322 2000
940.53' 18'092—dc21
[B]                                            99-33995
                                                        CIP

*In memory of my father and mother,
Beno and Sala Landau; my sister, Karin,
and my husband's parents, Julius and Julie Eichengreen,
all of whom perished in the Holocaust.*

# ❧ Contents ❧

# Preface

Chaim Rumkowski, the Elder of the Lodz Ghetto from 1940 to 1944, was and still is a very controversial figure.

During World War II the Germans established ghettos throughout Eastern Europe. The inhabitants of these ghettos were European Jews. The Germans also appointed an "Elder" for each ghetto, who had to follow and execute German orders.

The actions of Rumkowski, Elder of the ghetto Lodz (Litzmannstadt), differed greatly from those of the Elders in the ghettos of Warsaw, Kovno, Brezezy, or Pabianice.

I met Rumkowski when I was seventeen years old. I worked for him, I got to know him, and I feared for my life.

*Lucille Eichengreen*

# Acknowledgments

My deep thanks go to my many friends and family, without whose encouragement this book would not have been possible. I especially wish to thank Rebecca Camhi Fromer, who unselfishly listened to and worked with me through all phases of this work. Seymour Fromer gave freely of his time and compassion; Helmut Cohn, Fritz Hirschberger, Bernie Scharlach, Adrian Schreck, Felicia Weingarten, and Irith Altschuler-Zmany assisted me with their suggestions, and Tom Christensen and Kirsten Janene-Nelson, both of whom are on the staff of Mercury House, patiently awaited and received the text with insight and attention, easing its passage into publication.

# RUMKOWSKI

## and the Orphans of Lodz

אם אמרו להם עובדי כוכבים תנו לנו אחד מכם
ונהרגנו ואם לאו נהרוג כולכם.
יהרגו כולם ואל ימסרו להם נפש אחת מישראל.

If the idolators say:
"Hand over one of you and we will kill him;
or we will kill all of you."
Then let all be killed
but do not hand over even one soul of Israel.

*From the Mishnah Torah by Maimonedes*

*New Arrivals*

## ◆ *Initiations* ◆

My FATHER WAS AN INTELLIGENT, GREGARIOUS, and devoted man who loved life and prized his family above all else in the world. Neither my mother, my sister, Karin, nor I could imagine being without him . . .

We had no way of knowing, when the German army invaded Poland on September 1, 1939, and my father was arrested as a Polish national living on German soil, that we would never see him again. From that time on, he was imprisoned in the concentration camps at Fuhlsbuettel, Sachsenhausen, and Dachau. My mother tried to free him but all her efforts failed, and on January 31, 1941, we got the news that he had been killed in Dachau. The Gestapo informed us that he had died of pneumonia—but the few people we knew who had been released from Dachau told us of the beatings, starvation, and outright murder that were everyday occurrences there. The unimaginable, unwanted, and unsought truth had to be faced.

Several months after learning of my father's death, we received written orders from the Gestapo to prepare to leave within forty-eight hours. We were shipped out of Hamburg like objects, and arrived in Lodz, Poland, some time in October of 1941. Our destination was the ghetto—and from the very beginning of our stay there, life was chaotic, depressing, and frightening.

The ghetto in Lodz was closed off from the world with barbed wire, and we lived in isolation, surrounded by armed guards, in the former Balut section of the city. This area, which had been the poorest, most run-down district of this large industrial city, now "accommodated" Jews who were essentially captives. Before the war, thieves, black marketeers, and other unsavory characters lived among hard-working, honest Jews and Christians, but once the war began, the Christians were made to leave.

Food was scarce from the time we arrived until the time of our departure. Once a day, a crew of kitchen workers distributed a thin, watery soup—devoid of nourishment—a thin slice of bread, and a vile, bitter-tasting liquid called coffee; this was all we had to eat and, in time, our hunger ruled our lives and became the sole focus of our existence. We went to almost any length to get something edible, a bite to eat, rancid or not, and still we were hungry.

For more than six weeks, we—parents and children, young and old—slept on the cold, bare classroom floors of a deserted schoolhouse; after that, we were assigned to various rooms throughout the ghetto. With so many people forced to live in the ghetto, as many as seven to ten individuals had to share a single room. We had no running water, although we had access to a pump in the courtyard and could carry buckets of water upstairs. Indoor toilets belonged to another life; here, the outhouses were three flights down. As hunger weakened us, it became an ordeal to go up and down the stairs—and especially so during the middle of the night. Since many of us suffered from dysentery, it was often impossible to reach the outhouses in time—and then, of course, we endured humiliating accidents.

Upon the assignment of rooms, we qualified for individual ration cards; the food allotments were sporadic and meager, but my mother and sister and I did not complain. Hunger had silenced us, and we could only guess at one another's pain. Agony and loneliness, hunger and desperation had made us mute, but we were far from alone in our misery. Long lines of hungry ghetto dwellers waited outside the food distribution centers for hours on end before they got their meager rations. Hunger upon hunger was followed by even more hunger. The ghetto children grew hollow-eyed and thin; the adults became swollen and gaunt, and death stalked everyone.

Messages and orders, seldom good tidings or cheerful news, were posted on the walls of buildings throughout the ghetto. These notices, which were erratic and unpredictable, generally announced the current distribution of food—always less than the last posting—and carried the lists of names of those slated for deportation by the Germans. The Germans issued the orders and Chaim Rumkowski, who had been arbitrarily appointed the Elder by the Germans, implemented them. Work schedules for the various factories, as well as other newsworthy items, were also posted. Surprisingly, I can still recall one of these notices, which read:

AS OF NOVEMBER 3, 1941, THE DAILY BREAD RATION WILL BE REDUCED FROM 33 GRAMS TO 28 GRAMS; THIS IS CAUSED BY THE INCREASE IN THE GHETTO POPULATION 20,000 NEW ARRIVALS FROM THE WEST.

It was signed by C. Rumkowski, *Aeltester der Juden*, Elder of the Jews.

In those days, tears of sadness, anger, frustration, and sheer weakness often streamed down my face. Never had I felt so alone among so many other people, and never had I been so totally confused. I was sixteen; my mother, Karin, and I had four roommates, and yet I felt friendless. I had no one to talk to, and I certainly had no one in whom I could confide. How could I share my thoughts about the hopelessness of our situation, and add to our misery?

One day, as I pressed my tear-stained face against the cold windowpane of our room on Pawia 26, I caught sight of my mother down below. She wore her blue coat and a kerchief about her head, as she haggled with two women over a silk blouse in her hands. An hour later she came home without the blouse but with a package wrapped in an old newspaper. She did not say a word, but she looked happy. Before long, she unwrapped the package and spread a piece of margarine on two thin slices of bread: one for me, and one for Karin. I knew what she had done, but dared not say anything.

A few days after having witnessed this episode, I took my cue from my mother. I posted myself in the same courtyard but close to the wall of the building, so that my mother could not see me. From this position, I hoped to trade my alligator purse for a piece of bread. Although beautiful, costly, and even valuable under other circumstances, it had now become less important than our basic sustenance.

A young woman took an interest in the purse and came up to me. "I'm Luba," she said. "Let's see the bag." She checked the outside of the purse first and then opened it, found the little mirror within, and snapped the purse shut. I looked at her. She was about my age or a little older, short and plump, with dark, sparkling eyes, and a ready smile. Her hair, which was long and dark, rested on her shoulders. "How much do you want for the bag?" she asked, and I replied I wanted bread for it.

Luba's companion, a tall, well-dressed, good looking man of about thirty-five, took a wedge of bread out of his satchel and held it out to me, but I shook my head. "That is not enough," I said. "I will wait for someone else."

Luba and the man I had heard her call Genek whispered to one another briefly, and then walked away; twenty minutes later, however, they returned. "You are still here. The bag did not sell." Luba laughed cruelly and tears of anger welled in my eyes, but I restrained myself and did not speak. I knew she wanted the purse, and how much we needed the bread. When Genek removed two wedges from his satchel, I reached for them. The exchange had been made, the transaction was over, and I ran into the house, removing myself from Luba as quickly as I could. I did not like her, and never wanted to see her again. She had bread, as well as the power and protection of a man such as Genek at her side—and I had no taste for taunts.

Once in our room, I placed the bread on a shelf next to our few provisions. Of late, small quantities had been missing—a bit of bread one time, a little sugar or margarine another—and so I knew it was both risky and naive to hope no one would take the bread after I left—but the room was far from a sanctuary to me, and I had to get out of there. The room, small to begin with, seemed to shrink with each passing day, and I had begun to feel the walls closing in on me. With six others in it almost all the time, I had begun to feel as trapped as a caged animal. Mother and Karin generally huddled together under a blanket, which worried and depressed me, and our roommates, when not sullen, talked about food incessantly, which enraged me. They dwelled upon the past, upon what had been available before the war, and they dreamed aloud about the foods and delicacies they would eat after the war. In this way, they increased both their torment and ours. And so to escape, though the day was cold and rainy, I practically fled from the room and went out for a walk.

For the past several weeks I had devoted all my waking hours toward looking for a job—any job at all—in a factory, shop, or office. But I had no luck, and I had no connections. It was said, and rightfully so, that one had to have *plaices* or *protectectzia* in the ghetto, and this meant that one needed connections, or someone's shoulders "to stand on." When, on my walk, I came to the corner of Rybna and Lutomierska Streets, I noticed a small pushcart with a display of needles, thread, yarn, ribbons, combs, and other items. The owner of these goods stood behind his pushcart. He was about fifty and he wore a dark coat with fur collar and a felt hat—but what struck me most was that he waved and smiled as I passed him. From that time on, I made it a practice to walk past the pushcart. Once in a while I noticed he was with a young woman who called him Papa—and in this way I knew that he was not entirely alone.

About a week later, it just so happened that I needed a needle and black thread with which to sew the hem of my skirt. I welcomed the opportunity to stop at the pushcart, and when I did, the man looked at me and smiled as before, but this time he held out his hand too. "My name is Shlomo Berkowicz," he said. "I am standing here selling the remnants of my large pre-war store in Lodz. You can usually find me here in the afternoon; in the morning I work at the lumberyard. Employed persons get a daily bowl of watery soup; it has no nourishment value whatsoever, but it does the job of filling one's stomach temporarily." All this burst out of him in a steady stream—then he was silent.

I acknowledged what he had said with a nod, for I was quite shy, picked out a spool of thread and a needle, and asked: "How much?" When he replied, "Ten marks," though, I was shocked.

"I'm sorry, but I haven't got ten marks." Shlomo Berkowicz laughed. "I don't mean ten German marks! I mean ten *Rumkies!*"

My mother and I had the few German marks we had brought along with us from home, but we had little experience with the Rumkowski bills that we were given in change whenever we were able to buy a little "extra" food. I understood little about the currency in the ghetto. Shlomo took it upon himself to explain: "A German mark is worth ten times the value of the Rumkowski mark, but in the ghetto the Rumkowski mark is all we can use—at least technically. Even with 'real' money, however, it would make little difference, since there is hardly anything to buy."

"I have heard of Rumkowski, but who is he?" I asked eagerly. I had been in the ghetto for about six chaotic weeks and had scarcely spoken to anyone, so I didn't know much about how things were run.

"You must have seen the announcements and posters on buildings and posts throughout the ghetto! They are all signed by Rumkowski! He is the head of the *Judenrat,* or Jewish Council."

I wanted to hear more, but I did not want to appear stupid. I excused myself with a few short words, saying: "It's getting late," paid with a Rumkowski bill, and left. In a few days, I returned. I hesitated, then asked Shlomo to

*Ghetto money: one- and five-mark vouchers*

tell me more about Rumkowski, the ghetto, and its people. I had at last arrived at a point where I wanted to become integrated into my new situation. I hated to stick out; I was a Jew like the others, and yet I did not belong. I needed to know where I was, and I was eager to learn. *With whom had I been cast?* I had never seen anyone anywhere like those around me, and never before had I experienced conditions that even remotely resembled those in the ghetto.

Shlomo nodded his head knowingly. His language

poured over me in a medley of Polish, German, and Yiddish:

"Little is known about Rumkowski's past. He was born in 1877 in the village of Ilino, Russia. We know nothing about his parents or family other than the fact that his brother Jozef and his sister-in-law Helena are also in the ghetto. As a child he supposedly went to *Cheder,* a Hebrew school for young children—and it seems that he attended elementary school for about four years. He arrived in Lodz at the turn of the century. During the twenties and thirties, he was affiliated with the Zionist movement, but he was never held in high esteem, and he never became a leader.

"They say Rumkowski is a quarrelsome man, difficult to get along with. He has a reputation for being unpleasant. Although he likes to hear himself speak and often interrupts others, he seems to have gained entry into many of the Jewish organizations in town. He's been connected to the Jewish orphanages and has raised funds for them, but over the years many rumors have circulated about him."

As Shlomo spoke, my father's patience with me and my never-ending questions came to mind, and I was spellbound. When I asked him what he meant by "the rumors," I was no longer inhibited.

"I will be happy to tell you more, young lady, but it is a long story and you will have to return many more times." Shmuel laughed; we were becoming friends, and I felt free to think of him by his Yiddish name.

"As long as you are willing to talk to me, I will come whenever you have time."

"Time?" Shmuel saddened visibly. "I am a lonely, old man. Apart from time and memories, I have nothing."

I visited my new friend as often as I could, and he was always pleased to see me. "I have only one daughter; my wife died five years ago," he said. "I too am lonely, and I enjoy talking to you."

Shmuel's manner always touched me, and I eagerly awaited our visits. I longed for him to tell me what he knew and, in a way, he became my mentor. "I want to learn," I cried.

On a night I remember well, he said: "You will have to listen in installments; it is a long tale." And so saying, he pulled a small stool out from below the cart and motioned for me to sit. The gray evening dusk was settling around us and an early, cool autumn breeze made us shiver. We pulled our coats tightly around our bodies, and then he spoke:

"Let me begin with 1939, when the war broke out and Hitler invaded Poland. At that time I lived on Narutowica Street, as did a close friend of mine by the name of Sergei. We saw one another every day. We shared confidences. Both of us belonged to the *Bund,* a Jewish Socialist organization, but Sergei was also a member of the *Sejm*— which is a parliamentary body. Everyone respected him. I can remember one incident that will tell you a great deal about the regard in which Sergei was held by even the most unlikely of non-Jews in Lodz.

"As a rule, Sergei went everywhere by streetcar. One day, as he returned from the Balut, he noticed with dismay that his silver pocket watch was gone. On his thirteenth birthday his father had given him this watch, which was attached to a silver chain—and he had worn it from that day on. As he grew older, the silver chain could barely stretch across his ample stomach, but he continued to wear it with pride. It was the only memento he had that reminded him of his father, who had died when he was barely fourteen. Knowing the city well—and especially the Balut section of town—he concluded that one of the city's many pickpockets had made off with it while he was on the streetcar.

"Sergei wanted that watch back more than anything, but what was he to do? He decided to return to the Balut and, once there, go into one of the busiest bars in the district. There, he sought out the 'chief of pickpockets,' as they called him, and poured out his story. Stasz, "the chief"—a middle-aged, short and stout, ragged and dirty man with a conspicuously red face—smelled of vodka, but he was a good sort.

"Stasz patted Sergei on the shoulder and said: 'Don't worry. I'll get the watch back to you.' But when Sergei wanted to know how this could be achieved, Stasz's only reply was: 'Don't give it a thought. If I make a promise, it's a done deal.'

"The next morning when Sergei opened the door to his apartment, he discovered his watch wrapped in dirty paper. Later on, he was to learn that Stasz had issued orders that the watch be returned, and these orders were passed from one mouth to another. After that, anyone caught with Sergei's watch on his person had better fear for his life. Stasz's orders were the law of the Balut, and no one dared cross him. Sergei was happy and thankful. It meant a great deal to him that even in the Balut his name counted for something."

It was now completely dark and bitterly cold, and Shmuel rose. "I will tell you more when we meet again. It is just too cold, and I am hungry and tired."

Grateful for his story and companionship, I promised to come back soon. We shook hands; Shmuel packed up the pushcart, and I went to the freezing, overcrowded, ugly room I hated so much.

By the end of November I was at last lucky enough to find a job as a clerk-typist in an office on Rybna 8. I now qualified for the extra soup at lunchtime, but even so my hunger persisted. By eight in the evening, when I came "home" from work, it was already dark, and Shmuel was no longer at his accustomed post. So the next time I saw him I explained that I was working—and apologized for not having been able to see him—but Shmuel was happy for me and looked pleased.

"I am glad you have a job! This means you get a noonday soup! From now on, come to my room straight from work. We will not be much warmer there, but as we will be out of the wind at least we won't shiver." And so saying, he handed me a slip of paper with his address on it: Lutomierska 44. It was close to my office, and not far from the room on Pawia Street.

"I'll come to see you after work and, if you're not too tired, we can continue. But I can only stay about half an hour."

"I understand," he said. "Come when you can." From then on, we visited two or three times a week.

Not only did Shmuel have a larger room than ours, but he also owned some pre-war furniture, including a dresser, two beds, a table, and two chairs. In addition to these "luxuries," he and his daughter were the only ones assigned to the room. I relished the privacy we enjoyed as we sat at the table, shivering despite Shmuel's prediction, wrapped in our coats and wearing gloves for warmth, which were but little help in the sub-zero cold. "Where were we? How far did we get into the story?" Shmuel asked.

"You were speaking about Sergei and his watch." I was eager for him to go on. "What happened next?"

"At the end of August of 1939, I began to suspect that

*Midday soup*

Sergei was facing many difficult problems. He was unusually quiet and very pensive, and I got the impression that whatever it was, he had been wrestling with these matters for a long time. When I met with him one morning, he looked exhausted, and it was obvious to me that he had not slept very well. When I questioned him, he said: 'I have been staring at the dark ceiling all night long, trying to come to terms with myself. By dawn I had not only jumped out of bed, but also washed, dressed, and had coffee. And now, in my briefcase, I have a cleanly typed document that has to be taken downtown today. I am going to file a complaint with the authorities and request a formal hearing.'"

Shmuel paused. He wanted me to feel the suspense of that moment in 1939, and I did not disappoint him. I sat on the edge of my chair, waiting for him to continue.

"Sergei finally explained. 'The single sheet of paper in my briefcase weighs heavily on my mind and heart. It is no easy matter for a Jewish Councilman to file a complaint against one of his own.'"

Once more, Shmuel paused for effect before going on. "I can still hear Sergei's words. I remember he said: 'Since March, I have searched my conscience, and I have come to the conclusion that I must return to the orphanage. I want to talk to the children, and I want to get their story down on paper. Last spring, one of the girls from the Helenowek orphanage came to see me in my office. Her name was Luba, and she was about sixteen. She hesitated as she told me that she, as well as a younger girl and a boy, all of whom have been in the orphanage for several years, had been molested by one of the adults there. Reluctantly, and in tears, she finally stammered out the words: "The director ... Chaim Rumkowski ...," She hesitated, and then she sobbed—but the poor girl did not have a handkerchief with which to dry her tears, and so she used the sleeve of her patched sweater. I gave her an apple from my lunch bag and tried to calm her down. She was a pretty little thing, with dark brown eyes and dark hair—and she looked at me with such trust that I was moved to pity.

"'She stammered and explained that he touched her; that he did things to her that were not right—and then she began to cry again. I did not know what to say or do; and I did not have the nerve to ask any questions. To be truthful, I did not know what questions to ask! Although I am thirty-three years old, I have never heard anyone mention such matters before, but I consider the abuse of a child to be a serious matter ...

"'The room was quiet, and Luba looked at me. Finally, I rose from my chair, walked the girl to the door, and said that I would go to the orphanage to talk to her and

the others who had a similar complaint. That incident occurred in March, and I subsequently interviewed Luba,
eleven-year-old Bronia, and thirteen-year-old Julek. The
children's stories rang true, but they were very frightened.
They evidently had been threatened at the orphanage and
had been warned against speaking out.'

"As I looked at Sergei, I saw him in a new light. As if
for the first time, I noticed how short he was, how kind the
expression in his blue eyes was, what a gentle voice he had.

"Sergei took a deep breath and continued: 'Luba, at
fifteen, already understood that what had taken place was
neither right nor decent. Aside from talking to me, she
dared not confide in anyone. She told me she had lost her
parents at an early age and could barely remember them;
she showed me several old, faded photographs of them.
There were no other relatives, and by now she seemed to
have accepted her fate. She was proud that she was old
enough to work in the kitchen, that she could mop the
floors or wash the dishes. She had an infectious smile and
a sense of humor, but she said that she often cried at
night, that she buried her face in an old, smelly, tear-
stained pillow and thought aloud about the older ones
who had left the orphanage. She wondered where they
were, if they were happy—and I had no reply for her.'

"For some time Sergei sat quietly. Then he remembered little Bronia, a bright, intelligent girl of eleven who
happened to be a dwarf. He remembered how she looked
at him, and her low voice as she told her story: 'I lost my
mother when I was three, and neither my father nor older
brother or sister was willing or able to take care of me. My
father simply placed me in the orphanage, saying he was
too poor to feed another mouth. It took a long time to get
used to the orphanage, and to a life filled with rules and

*don'ts,* but I love being in the company of other children. I will never grow as tall as they are, but I can laugh and make sure that my short legs learn to run faster than theirs do so that I can keep up with them.' Sergei looked at her, and saw her pain.

"Sergei asked Bronia about Rumkowski, and she too burst into tears. Once she had calmed down, she stammered: 'Rumkowski took me by the hand, and led me to a small room in the back of the building. He lifted me up and made me stand on a chair; he told me to take off my skirt and panties, and then he touched me.' She sobbed, and refused to go beyond that point. Like the others, she had been threatened, and she, too, feared what might happen to her if anyone knew she had told him at least part of her story.

"Sergei seemed to be in shock. He paused before continuing: 'The entrance, the hallways and rooms in the boys' section of the orphanage were dark and dismal— and so I waited impatiently to speak to Julek. When he finally entered, I saw that he was a blue-eyed blond and tall for his age. He scrutinized me intently before speaking, with much difficulty and a severe stutter. He told me that he lived with his parents and older sister in Piotkow, not too far from Lodz. Because he stuttered and was different from the other children, his parents had sent him to the orphanage. At first the family had visited occasionally—but soon they began to neglect him, and finally he stopped hearing from them altogether. They were poor, and did not always have enough to eat at home. Four of them lived in a single room, and the father worked as a cobbler repairing shoes. Julek took a deep breath. He said that boys are not supposed to cry—that nothing really mattered, that he could take care of himself. Every word he uttered was tortured as a result of his affliction, and he did not sound convincing to me, but I got the feeling that he was proud to have made his statement.

"'As he stood before me, he was both frightened and embarrassed to tell his story. He acknowledged that on several occasions he had misbehaved in class and had been reported to the director. The usual punishment for minor infractions was a thrashing with a ruler, but instead he had been taken to the back room, where the director had asked him to remove his trousers. Then he touched him. As I listened to the boy, he blushed with shame. Over and over again he repeated that these were not things that were supposed to happen to boys.

"'After much investigative work and several additional interviews, I became convinced that the children were telling the truth. I was filled with abhorrence. Yet when I confronted the teachers and supervisors—threatening them with dismissal if they retaliated against the children—they were outraged and denied everything. One teacher stated categorically that the children's stories were pure invention. Still, my gut feeling was that all was not right, and that either an official hearing or an investigation would be needed to sort this out.'

"All this took place several months ago. When Sergei and I went together to the offices of the social welfare department with his complaint, we noticed that the clerk paid no attention to the contents of the single sheet we presented to him. He simply entered the complaint into a ledger, stamped it with a three-digit number, and promised to schedule an official hearing some time late in September. We breathed a sigh of relief as we walked out into the street, but we soon were filled with an uneasiness. Though we walked into the sunshine, we could not ignore the feeling of foreboding sweeping over us. Something frightening was hovering over us; something terrible and totally beyond our control was overtaking us."

Shmuel was tired. It was late, and I got up. It was time for me to return to my room.

"Remind me to tell you about September 1, 1939, the next time." Yes, Shmuel "enjoyed" speaking of the past.

"I will," I said, but I added: "It is a difficult story to understand."

Shmuel nodded. "Believe me, it's a true story." At that we shook hands, and I rushed out of the house into the night.

I was about to cross the street when I heard the clacking of hoofbeats. Even in the darkness I could make out the forms of a mottled gray horse, a driver on a high perch, and—seated within the carriage—Rumkowski, staring straight ahead. I wondered what kind of a man he was, and if he really molested the children in the orphanage. Here was a man who had power over the entire ghetto and all of our lives—and, ever so briefly, I envied him. I envied his unlimited control over the supply of food, while I was forever hungry and most certainly starving.

⤳⋇⤳

During the following week new food distributions were announced, and for the first and only time a meat ration of fifty grams was allocated for each person. After spending several hours in line, waiting to collect our rations, I learned that to get the meat I had to go to a store serving as a butcher shop. The next day passed—and, after work, I lined up at the designated place. Two hours later, those of us who had waited for our turn were told all the meat had been distributed and we would have to return the follow-

ing day. We had been out in the freezing cold, and many
men and women shouted in frustration and anger. They
cursed the butcher and they cursed the ghetto—but most
of all, they cursed Rumkowski. When I went back to my
room, I was resigned, tired, and hungry. I knew that on
the following day I faced the prospect of going through
the same ritual once again. I would stand in line and hope
for our meager ration of meat.

The next night the line was a little shorter, and I
guessed that most of the people who had arrived before
me had collected their allotment. Finally, when my turn
came, I received a small package—a large, lean bone. The
"meat" on it was dark red or burgundy in color, and
looked peculiar. I had never seen anything like it before.
The man alongside me saw how perplexed I was and
looked straight at me. In a voice full of disgust, he spat
out a single word: "Horsemeat!"

Hunger was taking its toll. In the twelve months since
our arrival in the fall of 1941, my sister had become quiet
and very unlike the lively child I once knew, and my
mother's legs and feet were so swollen she barely managed to drag them along whenever she tried to walk. We
no longer cared what we ate, and it no longer made any
difference what I brought with me as part of our ration.
We simply cooked it for a long time in a little water, until
we ran out of our coal ration. When we were able to get
meat, it proved to be tough—but it did not matter. We
divided scraps, chewed stringy meat, and downed sweet-
tasting horsemeat. Neither Karin nor Mother made any
comments, and I never told them what they ate . . .

The next evening, I went to see Shmuel. "I was to tell
you about September 1, 1939," he said.

"On September 1, 1939, everyone in Lodz was glued to
the radio to hear the 'unbelievable news.' Our foreboding

of several weeks' duration had become a reality. Germany had attacked, and massive German armies had invaded Poland. The Polish army resisted fiercely. And two questions were on everybody's minds: will Poland be able to repel the Germans? Can the Polish people oust the enemy from its territory? Hopes were high—but in the days that followed, the news became very alarming. The Germans were occupying city after city. Seven days after the invasion, they had occupied most of Poland, including the large cities and industrial centers. The war was lost for Poland.

"A few short days later, the Germans concentrated on the Jews. Bearded Jews, as well as some women and children, were special targets. Men were beaten, and their beards and sidelocks were shorn. They were humiliated; they were forced into labor battalions. At times they were made to scrub the sidewalk with toothbrushes; quite often they were shot without provocation. The Jews of Poland had heard of the maltreatment suffered by their brothers in Germany, and yet they were stunned. Men who belonged to Zionist organizations or who held prominent posts in the community were arrested. During the succeeding weeks, and particularly because of the nature of these events, some decided to flee and leave all possessions behind—but when they tried to leave the country, they discovered that Poland's borders were closed. A very few managed to get out via legal channels and with the proper documentation, but others escaped toward the east and headed for the Russian border. Many Jews in the larger cities decided to 'wait and see.' They waited to find out if they could actually lead a normal life under the Germans."

"What did Sergei decide to do?" I asked.

"At first, Sergei was at a loss. Some of his friends

advised him to stay, and others urged him to leave at once—regardless of direction. 'Just try to escape,' they counseled, but Sergei had just gotten married a few weeks earlier, and neither he nor his wife, Betty, could decide what to do. In the end, they too opted to 'wait and see.' They packed two small bags and waited; if they had to leave at a moment's notice, they would be ready.

"A week later the Germans came looking for Sergei— Sergei and my family lived in the same apartment house. Both he and Betty were visiting friends at the time—but on their return, they knocked on my door. I told them they were wanted by the Gestapo, and we embraced a last time. They had decided to hide at a friend's house, and promised to send some kind of word to me."

Shmuel and I had a drink of hot water, and then he continued.

"Lodz was rampant with rumors, but by October 1939, most of the Jews had heard that the Germans wanted to set aside special areas for them throughout Poland. A ghetto—it was said—but nothing seemed definite. One morning, the Germans burst into the Jewish Community House and pointed at random to a gray-haired man with slightly stooped shoulders: *'Du bist jetzt der Aeltester der Juden in Litzmannstadt,'* (You are now the Elder of the Jews in Litzmannstadt). Everyone was stunned. The Germans had picked Rumkowski to head the *Judenrat,* and had renamed the area.

"At the time, Rumkowski still worked for the Jewish orphanage in Lodz; he raised funds for its support—but we would still hear rumors about his molestation of the children, especially the girls.

"As soon as Sergei learned of the proposed ghetto and of Rumkowski's appointment as its head, he both anticipated and feared the retaliation that was due to come on account of his role in spearheading the investigation of the orphanage. The following day he and Betty took their bags and hoped to cross the border into Russia. Meanwhile the ghetto was to be run by Jews, who were not only to keep order within but also were 'obliged' to follow German orders. In reality, the Germans controlled the life of the ghetto from their own headquarters in the city.

"The German orders for the creation of the ghetto were made public in December 1939. They specified that the Jews of Lodz were to leave their homes and move to the Balut. Only a few Jews understood that in the future they would be called upon to share a single room with many others, or that their 'accommodations' would have no running water, toilets, central heat, or provision for the use of a simple gas stove. The impact of the 'new life' was evident to all by the first of May in 1940, however, for this was the cut-off date for all Jews to move.

"They carried their belongings and pushed their wagons and carts. The latter were laden with household goods and anything else that could be salvaged in the short time allotted for the move. The affluent came with their goods on trucks, but much of their property had to be left behind. Among the poorer households, the 'bread-givers' were left behind . . ."

"What do you mean by a breadgiver?" I interrupted.

Shmuel explained: "For many years before the war, poor families worked in the textile mills. They earned very little and barely provided for daily necessities. To supplement their income, they borrowed money to either buy or lease weaving looms. These looms were often brought into the tiny, cramped quarters where the entire family lived—parents, children, and in some cases even animals. Although they worked hard by night, these poor souls received so meager a wage that they barely had enough to

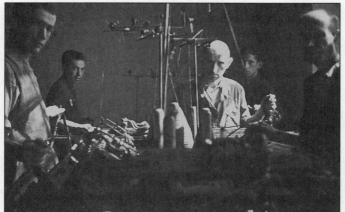

*Knitting Factory, Lodz Ghetto*

© Jüdisches Museum, Frankfurt

make the installments on the loom. Despite the travail and doubtful outcome of the efforts involved in these desperate moves to support one's self and family, the loom was ironically referred to as 'breadgiver' in Yiddish."

I had grown up in a comfortable, middle-class home, and I found it hard to absorb the account of such abject poverty. When I raised this point to Shmuel, he looked at me. "Believe me," he said, "the deprivation here was greater than that. I know you have no idea of what it's like to live under these conditions." He was very sad when he sighed: "*Ach.* The standards you knew in Western Europe were only a dream for most of us!"

It was later than I thought. I excused myself hurriedly, promising to return soon . . . Our visits had become a vital part of my life, and by now I had little doubt that Shmuel's stories filled in my world as once books, the movies, and my absent father had.

Almost a week passed. Mother was weak and listless; Karin was frightened. I dropped in on Shmuel in my accustomed manner. Immediately upon my entering the room he saw how strained and troubled I was. Pulling out a chair for me, he asked if I was concerned about my mother. I nodded, and the room fell silent. After a while, however, Shmuel proposed that we go on. "Let me tell you about the summer of 1940." He was unfailingly kind, and given the state I was in, I welcomed the chance to focus on what he was about to say.

"In May 1940, the ghetto was surrounded by barbed wire, and we were completely closed off from the outside world. Rumkowski set about the business of organizing a ghetto council and found a number of decent people willing to serve responsibly. Among them were Eliasz Tabaksblat, Mosze Karo, Henryk Neftalin, and many others. Most of them were educated people of conscience who had a genuine desire to establish manageable living conditions within the ghetto. Unfortunately, several unsavory characters were brought in as well. Since Rumkowski had enormous power and made many of the decisions himself, no one dared interfere with him. In no time at all those who had argued with or opposed him began to fear for their lives. Rumkowski often inquired about Sergei and seemed to know about the complaint lodged against him with the Polish authorities. Now that he was in control of the ghetto, he wanted to crush Sergei. He wanted to avenge himself, and he wanted to impress everyone with the power resting in his hands. He looked everywhere for Sergei, but as it so happened, no one knew of his whereabouts. Rumkowski made threats and offered bribes, but he got nowhere."

"What happened to the children?" I asked.

"Some were transferred to the orphan asylum in Marysin, but a few older ones made their own plans. I know very little about the three children Sergei spoke of.

Luba came into the ghetto; she lives in a small room and actually may work in the same building you work in, but I am not sure about that. Julek disappeared. No one has seen or heard of him; and since he did not come into the ghetto, my guess is that he ran away. The youngest, Bronia, moved into the ghetto with her father, brother, and sister. She shares a room with them. The family is not happy to have her, but since she is the only one who works, they endure her."

Shmuel dozed off in exhaustion, and I left quietly.

In the days that followed, Shmuel no longer went out to sell his wares from the pushcart. He was thin, weak, listless, and bloated—and yet he gathered what little energy he had to drag himself to the lumberyard every day; as a worker, he was entitled to the daily ration of watery soup, and he struggled to stay alive. When I managed to see him, I would find him in bed. Directing me to be seated, he continued to tell me what he knew about the ghetto. We carried on as before, and acted as if nothing had changed. "Have you read Rumkowski's latest statement?" he asked. "'Nothing will happen to people of good will and only work can save us.'" He did not wait for me to reply.

"I detest Rumkowski and his senseless statements. They are frustrating and unacceptable to us, but they please the Germans. I hate him, but I have to admit that he has a talent. He has organized the factories and shops in the ghetto, and the Germans keep us busy. We do the sewing, leatherwork, and woodwork—or whatever else is demanded of us—but we have a problem, a serious problem. When the Germans promise to send food into the ghetto, it is always marginal."

"Didn't they agree to send enough for everyone?" I asked.

"Of course not!" Shmuel laughed. "I don't have to tell

you how hungry we are and how little we have to eat. We are never free of hunger!"

Shmuel's energy ebbed; his eyes closed, and once more I left quietly, rushing through the dark, cold streets.

I came home to a mother who was weak and lethargic, and to a sister who was quiet—a little girl devoid of words, tears, laughter, or joy. I did not know what to do. How could I help either of them when what they needed most was food, and I could not provide that? No one had food and everyone suffered, but some of us did not have the strength to go on—and so, the pain of watching my mother and sister deteriorate ate away at me.

Spring came, and along with it came ongoing orders for massive deportations, which systematically depleted the ghetto. Everyone suffered, silently or otherwise, but the evacuations of the older Jews who had arrived from the Reich in October, 1941, were especially merciless. In a matter of a few weeks forty-five thousand Jews "disappeared." They "went to work" in Western Europe, and not a word from them ever reached us.

On July 13, 1942, at noon, my mother died while I was at work. My sister Karin was unaware that she had gone, and so I have assumed that she died quietly. Hers was a typical ghetto death: we had no tears, no family, and no friends to mourn with us. Karin had just "celebrated" her eleventh birthday, and I was sixteen. We had no one, and I was desperately lonely.

Four days after my mother died, I went to see Shmuel. I knocked on the door—and when his daughter opened it, I knew. Shmuel's bed was empty. "My father has been dead for two days," she said. "Hunger conquered his will to live. Toward the end, this once-happy, strong man did not not want to go on." "I'm sorry," I choked. I could not say another word; Mother and Shmuel were dead, and I was deserted and lost in a madhouse.

My mother's lethargy and Karin's remoteness had pained me more than words can express, and I had long before developed the habit of rushing home to make our meager meal—a turnip, or a turnip and a potato boiled in water to make it go further—and then escaping for the evening. I had needed to be with Shmuel. There, with him, we were mutually comforted; he as my teacher and I as his adoring pupil. He had been there for me. I shall never forget that.

I got Karin a job in a hat factory so that she could be with other children and qualify for a bowl of noonday soup. The children, listed as "workers," were, in fact, taught the rudiments of arithmetic, Hebrew, and Polish— but Karin's disposition did not change. She had closed herself off from the world, and not even I could penetrate the darkness into which she sank.

*A child eating in the ghetto*

## 2

### ❧ *Buried Conscience and Guilt* ❧

THE DAY AFTER MY MOTHER'S DEATH, I HAD TO RE-
turn to work. Coworkers touched my shoulder in sympa-
thy or hugged me, but I could not be comforted. My
swollen face said everything.

Dorka, who lived on the floor below us, began to look
in on us in our room. She read to Karin in Polish and
German, and talked to me about food rations and work.
Inevitably, we spoke about our lives before the war. I soon
began to feel as grateful as an orphan who had been
adopted, and appreciated how she watched over us.

Dorka was about fifty, a woman who characteristically dressed in black, gray, or brown; above all, she was a
woman of impeccable cleanliness. Six people shared her
room. She had no family, and she had no one close to her
in the ghetto. Her work in the straw factory consisted of
sewing large, heavy, straw braids into oversized shoes,
which were to be worn by the Germans over their boots
on the snow-covered Russian front. As a result, her fingers were always raw, bruised, and red from handling the
wet, stinging straw.

It did not take long for me to become accustomed to
Dorka's presence in our room. One day, after I asked what
she had done before the war, she said: "I taught in the

Jewish schools, but when the ghetto was established and some of the children who'd lost their parents were transferred to the orphanage in Marysin, I applied for work there. I had a brief interview with Rumkowski, and when he accepted me, I felt lucky."

"Did you take the job?" I asked.

"Yes. I worked from 1940 until 1941, when Rumkowski fired me for asking too many questions."

"What kind of questions did you ask?"

"What I'm about to tell you must never be repeated," she said. "Do you promise to say nothing to anyone?"

I nodded, and she proceeded:

"Let me start with the fall of 1940. Up until then, I had always worked with children. Here, in the ghetto, I was again fortunate to teach. I loved to see the young learn, and I was happy to be with them.

"The orphanage was situated in a large, plain house in need of paint both indoors and out. The rooms were small, and they were filled with cots for both the children and the staff. The kitchen was large enough, but there were no bathrooms or toilets. We used outhouses, and we hauled water indoors in large buckets from an outside pump. What furniture there was was sparse, but we made do. We knew that conditions elsewhere in the ghetto were far worse. We were painfully aware of the brutally cold winter, the absence of coal, and an ever-present hunger due to lack of food.

"Rumkowski at first saw to it that we had more food and coal than others, but after a few months he cut our rations. We were hungry, and the children cried out for food and sweets. They could not understand that we had none to give. It was heartbreaking to see their suffering as they starved.

"Early one morning, just after the orphanage had come into being, I heard a knock on the door. I opened it, and before me stood a tiny girl. She wore a blue coat and matching cap, and she carried a cardboard box. I ushered her in, asking what her name was. The child, Mania Zylbersztajn, was eight years old.

"'Where are your parents? Where is your family? Where do you come from?' I asked, trying to elicit some information, but she merely looked at me without saying a word. Her brown eyes were opened wide and her face was set in a serious manner, but she neither spoke to me nor responded when someone else tried to engage her."

"Did you let her stay?" I asked.

"Yes, but I knew that eventually Rumkowski would have to approve the step I had taken. Meanwhile, the children and I found that her cardboard box contained a small violin, several dresses, two extra pairs of shoes, underwear, and two books. We could not help but notice that her tailored coat was lined with white fur, and from this we inferred that she came from a wealthy family—but that is all we 'knew.' We could not persuade her to speak. No one recognized her, or had anything to tell us about her.

"Mania was exceptionally beautiful. She smiled frequently, and was a well-behaved, extremely bright girl. Given time, she began to express herself. She spoke, read, and wrote flawlessly, and coaxed her violin to play. She was an amazingly gifted child.

"Whenever I asked her where she had learned to play, her answer was no answer. With no leads to go on—no photographs and no names or addresses among her things—we finally accepted her as an 'abandoned child' and stopped asking questions.

"Rumkowski made regular visits. 'My children' is

what he called the orphans. He brought them hard candy—an almost unheard-of luxury in the ghetto—and the youngsters were thrilled. Of course, he could not help but notice Mania. She stood out among the other children because she was so beautiful—but she was also unusually polite, and did not behave like an ordinary child. Rumkowski inquired about her parents and her past, but he fared no better than we—Mania divulged nothing. She was an eight-year-old who either could not speak about the past or had been warned to never say anything about it. In no time at all, he singled her out; he patted her head, gave her several additonal pieces of candy, and held her hand. Mania thanked him with a smile.

"During his next visit a few weeks later, Rumkowski asked Mania to get her coat and put it on. He took her for a ride in his *droshki,* and she was delighted. She sat on his lap as the driver encouraged the horses to gallop, and she laughed aloud. When Rumkowski returned, he told Mania that he would come again. She looked forward to these visits and, inevitably, rumors spread: 'Rumkowski will probably adopt Mania; he likes her more than the others.' 'She is lucky Rumkowski is her benefactor,' etc. Everyone envied her for the special status she seemed to enjoy."

"What did you think?" I asked.

"I did not know what to think. All I know is that I felt uncomfortable, and began to worry. When I remembered the rumors about Rumkowski and the orphans at Helenowek, my concern grew.

"Rumkowski's visits continued. Winter came. It was bitter cold in the ghetto; the roads were covered with snow and ice, and Mania's excursions in the horse-drawn buggy came to an end. When Rumkowski came to the orphanage, he no longer brought sweets, but he joked and laughed and promised the staff he would give the children preferential treatment. If at all possible, he would see to it they got extra food. As it turned out, however, not even Rumkowski could achieve this.

"During his visit in December, he made himself comfortable in the director's office and asked that several children be sent in to him; he inquired about their schoolwork and praised those who got good grades on their papers. After an hour, he asked for Mania. She greeted him and smiled happily when she entered. Rumkowski took her by the hand and locked the door behind her. But soon we heard the child's shrill cries and agonized shrieks. We did not know what to do! Like fools and cowards, we dared not knock on the door—and so, we waited. When Rumkowski finally opened the door, he pushed a sobbing Mania out of the room in a distinctly rough manner.

"Mania's face was ashen, and streamed in tears. The right sleeve of her dress was torn at the seam, and in her bulging skirt pocket were her crumpled panties . . . I held her hand, and walked her to my room; I filled the wash bowl with warm water, undressed and bathed her. She could not stop trembling, and so I wrapped her in a large blanket and put her to bed. I held her by the hand, but neither of us spoke. Mania cried quietly, all the while clinging to my hand, and after a few hours she fell into a fitful sleep. I went to bed and held her close to me all night long.

"The next morning, Mania clung to my skirt and would not let me out of her sight. Days afterward, we noticed that she had changed markedly. She was withdrawn and had stopped playing the violin; and, although we pleaded with her, she refused to touch it. The staff knew very well that all was not right, but no one spoke to her or tried to find out what had brought about this sudden change. Everyone dreaded Rumkowski's anger and absolute power. My love and affection for her did not help.

"Six weeks later, Rumkowski's impending visit for the following day was announced. The floors were scrubbed and the rooms tidied up; the children were cleaned and bathed. Mania cried hysterically; she hit the other children, and behaved in such a strange manner that we thought she was either sick or unbalanced. We 'blindly' blamed this on the inadequate diet. Meanwhile, the children rehearsed a song for Rumkowski and were put to bed early; we wanted them to be fresh and rested for the visit.

"That night, I watched over Mania. She tossed and turned, but she could not sleep. By midnight, however, I was totally exhausted and went to my room. I slept a few hours—but as things turned out, I should have stayed with her.

"At breakfast time, Mania's chair was empty. We searched everywhere, neglecting nothing from the attic to the basement, but we could not find her. She had left everything behind, with the exception of her coat and hat, and we reasoned that she would return when she got hungry. The director cried: 'How am I going to explain to Rumkowski that the child is missing? Mania, of all children!' She was petrified, realizing that Mania's disappearance could cost her her job.

"At midmorning, I put my coat on; my head was covered in a cap and I wore heavy boots. At the back of the orphanage, I found small footprints in the fresh, glistening snow, and I followed them cautiously. The cold sun cast long shadows, and I kept on walking. I had nearly reached the outer limits of the ghetto, and the barbed wires that separated us from the rest of the population, when I came upon a German sentry who patrolled the area from the other side of the fence. He stood before a red-and-white striped hut, which we always referred to as a 'box,' and shouted 'Halt!' just as I was about to turn back. I stopped in my tracks.

"The sentry aimed his rifle at me. 'You there, come here!' I inched toward him, until only about two feet separated us. As I did so, however, I saw a small, crumpled heap and recognized Mania's blue coat. My heart beat furiously, and I nearly stopped breathing. Never before had I stood so close to a German, and never before had I been so afraid for my life. 'Pick up the body and take it away!' he ordered.

"I bent down and carefully lifted Mania. A few drops of blood had soaked into the snow, and on her forehead I saw a single, small, red hole. Mania was ice cold, and the strands of her dark hair were frozen stiff. I carried her back to the orphanage, put her on a bed, and closed the door behind me. I did not want the children to see her. Suddenly I became aware that the staff had crowded into Mania's room, surrounding her. I saw the director put her ear to Mania's mouth and feel for her pulse, but of course there was no sign of life. 'She probably got too close to the barbed wires, and the German shot her' was all she could think of saying. No one spoke about why she may have wanted to leave, but I could only assume that Rumkowski terrified her.

"When Rumkowski appeared, the director shook as she informed him of Mania's 'mishap.' Rumkowski was furious! He ranted and raved, called us imbeciles, and accused us of negligence. Over and over again he screamed: 'How could this have happened?' His face became beet red, and he wrung his hands.

"Rumkowski interviewed the staff individually, and when my turn came I said: 'Mr. President, Mania has not been the same since your last visit. She was disturbed, and cried continually.' At first, his eyes were ablaze with hatred, but then they narrowed. Trembling at the lips, he snarled at me: 'What are you implying?' His voice had now become hoarse and raspy. 'If you ever say anything like that again,' he threatened, 'I'll have you deported. Pack your things! Leave! Get out of my sight! As of tomorrow, you will work in the straw-shoe factory!'

"I left the room, packed my things, and began the long walk into the center of the ghetto. I spent that night with a former classmate and, as ordered, the next day I reported for work at the factory. Eventually, I found this place in which to stay—but the memory of Mania gives me no peace; it haunts me day and night. I blame myself for failing to help her, as well as for letting her out of my sight."

"What do you think really happened to Mania?" I asked.

Dorka remained silent for some time. Finally deciding to speak, she took a deep breath, and said: "What I am about to say could cost me my life—but I think Rumkowski abused her. After sobbing and brooding for weeks, Mania must have concluded that she could not face him again. She was afraid of him, and when Rumkowski's visit was announced, she could think of nothing better than escape."

Dorka broke down in tears, and pain contorted her face. "As long as I live, I will never forgive him for what he did—but some day, even he will have to account for his evil deeds." Cradling her head in her hands, she rocked back and forth. When she got up, she embraced me without saying a word, then left the room, utterly exhausted.

Once more, I had learned about a child who had suffered at Rumkowski's hands. Shmuel's story about Sergei and the investigation of 1939 could not be forgotten. I was afraid. I was afraid of the unknown, dark future, with Rumkowski at the head of the ghetto.

*Rumkowski in his horse-drawn carriage*

## 3

<es> *Corruption and Collusion* <es>

J ULY AND AUGUST, 1942, WERE HOT AND HUMID. Typhoid raged throughout the ghetto. Every room in every house seemed to be contaminated. We had no medication at all, and the ghetto hospital was out of the question. Every bed there was occupied, and cots, filled with the ailing, spilled out into the crammed corridors. Hunger and death stalked the ghetto at every turn, and most of us became discouraged. We had lost hope.

The mechanics of ghetto life rolled on and ran their usual course. Internal mail, and orders from the ghetto administration on Balucki Rynek, continued to be delivered to us. Every two days, a young, deformed woman with a pleasant face came to our office to pick up our reports of work performed to deliver to ghetto headquarters; she later returned with instructions for us from Rumkowski's office.

This messenger's name was Bronia, and she frequently stopped at my desk to talk to me. One day, in her typical, direct manner, she said: "I know that people find it hard to accept me as a dwarf. They either stare at me or ignore me completely, but I try to make up for my appearance by being helpful, happy, obliging, and efficient. That is how I behave—but what I really want are friends, not pity." Her words touched me, and I found myself saying: "May I be your friend?" I, too, desperately needed someone, and I suppressed the fact that her appearance bothered me.

Bronia stretched her hand out to me. When I took hold of it I was surprised by its strength. She sat down at once—and from then on, whenever she came, it was her custom to pull a chair close to me at my desk and spend an hour with me. No one dared approach or reproach her. She was Rumkowski's messenger, and under his protection.

During the ensuing weeks, I often pleaded with Bronia to tell me about her life and experiences. One day, she began:

"When I was two, my mother died. I hardly remember her now—but I do recall that at the time of her death we lived in a village about two hours' distance from Lodz. Our family consisted of my father, sister, brother, and myself. The house was old, and in need of repair. It was much too small for four people, since it just had one room with a single, narrow window. As you can imagine, we had very little furniture: a large bed, a table and two chairs, and that was it. The 'kitchen area' had three shelves and a rusty, metal stove. We had neither running water nor a toilet in the house. My father worked as a blacksmith, but he never had enough money to buy the food we needed to sustain us. He was—and still is—an angry man. Basically, he felt that life had dealt him a bad hand, and that he deserved better. Most of the time I was left alone at home; then, unexpectedly, when I was about three, the few things I had were thrown into a box. My father brought me to the Jewish orphanage at Helenowek and simply left me there. Neither he nor my sister or brother ever visited me. I lived among strangers, but I now had more to eat."

Bronia's voice broke; tears streamed down her face, and I was in shock. This was the first time I had heard of a parent willingly or callously giving up a child. Very much shaken, I asked her to tell me how much time, how much of her life, had been spent in the orphanage.

"I lived there until the beginning of the war," Bronia answered. "When there was talk of transferring everyone in the orphanage to the ghetto, I packed up and walked in. Now, when I think of the past, I have to admit that in some ways life was easier for me in the orphanage. I went to school; I learned how to read and write, and most of my classes were enjoyable. I was lonely, and it was difficult to adjust to institutional life, but it might have been bearable, were it not for Rumkowski.

"Rumkowski likes young girls," she whispered. "He called us into his office one at a time; he shut the door, and then he touched and fondled us. Since I was so small, he made me stand on a chair and ..."

Bronia could not go on; she was crying. Remembering Shmuel's story about Sergei's investigation of Helenowek, weeks before the onset of the war, I asked: "Didn't someone come to talk to the children and confront Rumkowski?"

"Just before the war a man named Sergei came to talk to me, to Luba, who now works on the second floor of this building, and to Julek, who ran away rather than come into the ghetto," she replied. "Sergei promised to file a complaint and assured us that Rumkowski would have to leave us alone—but the war broke out and nothing further happened. After that, the Germans ordered the ghetto established in the Balut. At the Jewish Community House, the Germans selected Rumkowski to be the Jewish head of the ghetto.

"I will always remember 1940 to 1941, my first winter

here. I was filled with anguish. I had come to the ghetto in order to get away from the orphanage, and I had joined my father, sister, and brother in their room. It was certainly no improvement over the pre-war house I had remembered—but now I had hunger, icy frost, and the indifference of my family to contend with as well. All of it was painful to bear.

"My father, brother, and sister taunted me constantly: 'Why don't you ask Rumkowski for help?' When I stubbornly refused, they vented their anger on me. At night in the dark, and to this day, I often wish I had never been born . . . Anyway, I found a job in one of the garment factories. I carried thread from machine to machine, and lugged large, heavy bundles of cut cloth to be made into coats for the German army."

Abruptly, without another word, Bronia rose, turned, and walked out of the room. I was surprised when she returned on the following day, taking her customary seat at my desk. Without prompting, she took up the threads of her story.

"With the help of a friend, I managed to find a job for my father in the felt-shoe factory, but for about a year neither my brother nor my sister were able to find work. They complained and grumbled incessantly, and blamed me for their misery and lack of food, as well as for the cold room in which we lived. As long as I have breath, I will never be able to understand why they hated me and resented my deformity. If only my mother had lived! How different my life would have been!"

She sighed, and went on: "On one of Rumkowski's frequent inspections, he spotted me at work in the garment factory. He remembered me from Helenowek, and immediately ordered me to see him at his office on

Balucki Rynek. The following day, he gave me a job as messenger. I was now considered a working member of the ghetto administration, and my food rations were increased. My family welcomed the additional food, and became friendlier than I had ever known.

"Since that meeting at the garment factory, I see Rumkowski quite often. Whether it is day or night, he makes sure that few clerks are in the headquarter barracks before he asks me to enter his office. Once the doors are shut, he victimizes me. I try to get away, but his iron grip on my arm fastens me to him. My tears and pleas do not move him; he remains indifferent, and even hostile. I am revolted when his groping hands touch me in places I cannot mention, and I cannot tolerate his smelly breath or the slobbering lips he presses to my face. I feel sullied, disgusted, and ashamed, because I am often reduced to the level of praying for his death." Bronia's voice broke: "If only I could run away," she cried.

"Don't you know anyone who can be trusted to talk to Rumkowski on your behalf?"

Bronia laughed sarcastically. "You are so naive! Don't you realize what will happen to me if I speak out or make trouble—or if this should become public knowledge? There are no reins on Rumkowski's anger, and there is no limit to his capacity for inflicting punishment or taking revenge. He is the most powerful person in the ghetto, and I am terrified of him."

I took hold of Bronia's hand, and held onto it. I could not make a single suggestion. I pitied her, and imagined I could feel her pain. By now, even I had come to know that not a single soul in the ghetto had the nerve to confront Rumkowski. There was no one who had the foolhardiness, courage, or daring to broach this subject. The rumors that had circulated before the war were resurfacing; they were of one cloth with Bronia's story—and yet, nothing would be done.

The last week in August, Bronia entered the building in a state of excitement. She stopped at my desk. "Rumkowski will make an important speech tomorrow. I have heard various rumors, but I cannot repeat them. I will report what I learn as soon as possible." I nodded. Whatever it was, it sounded ominous.

For days, the office had been filled with gossip about further deportations, but none of us could verify anything. On the day of Rumkowski's speech, what he said spread throughout the ghetto. Those who were not there received the news in total disbelief. But many had been present to hear Rumkowski's words in person, and there was no doubt about their authenticity. Rumkowski's message to the Jews of the Lodz ghetto was in part expressed in the following words:

> Brothers and sisters, fathers and mothers, hear me. Give me your children.... I was given orders by the Germans to send away twenty-four thousand Jews from the ghetto, and if I do not comply, the Germans will take charge. I managed to have them reduce the figure to twenty thousand. I must deport all children from two months to the age of ten, and if I don't, others will be taken too.

Those who were there gasped. Some cried: "How can you ask this of us?"; others shouted: "You ought to be ashamed of yourself!" Rumkowski continued:

> I tried to reduce the Germans' demand for us to turn over all children from the newborn to the ten-year-olds to include only those up to the age of nine, but

they would not yield. They insist upon deporting the
children under the age of ten, as well as the adults over
the age of sixty-five. We must give them our sick and
ailing, so that the rest of us can live . . .

I was in the office at the time of Rumkowski's speech and
did not hear him, but I did overhear the outcry of my
neighbors, coworkers, and people in the street. They
cried: *How dare he make such a request? Where are his
morals? Where is his compassion?*

When he was through, Rumkowski was pelted with
stones as he passed by in his horse-drawn carriage—but
of what possible use was that? He had made it only too
clear that he would cooperate with the Germans for the
sake of "the ghetto's good." The Jews of Lodz repeated his
words with anger, to no effect. In the end, approximately
twenty-five thousand human beings were to be deported,
as the Germans arbitrarily reduced or increased such fi-
gures at their whim.

At every possible turn Rumkowski pleaded for understanding, but what was there to understand? He had
asked us to cooperate with the Germans, and he had
asked us to surrender our aged and our young—but these
"requests" were beyond the reach of understanding. We
seethed in outrage, but we did not revolt. Incomprehensible as it may seem, no one dared oppose Rumkowski.

At every turn, the Germans found fault with the Jews
responsible for the administration of the ghetto, whom
they blamed for being "too slow" in implementing orders
or compiling the lists of those to be deported. They therefore claimed to "lose patience," and "justified" imposing a
*Sperre*—which is somewhat more than a curfew. In this
case, the *Sperre* involved the house arrest of everyone in
the ghetto, or well over a hundred thousand Jews. To dis-

seminate the news, proclamations were posted in key locations throughout the entirety of the area to the effect that from the 5th to the 12th of September 1942, no one was to report for work or leave his or her room. Seven whole days!

My sister was in danger, and her fate troubled me constantly. She was eleven—and, although Rumkowski had said the "older children" would not be deported, I wondered how I or anyone else could rely on his word. Karin was tall for her age, and I wanted to believe that she would be safe; I worked hard to convince myself that she would not be scooped up and pushed out of my life—but a small voice within nagged me, and raised the banner of fear.

Those of us who lived in our building spoke of hiding the old and the young, and speculated about what to say to the Germans when they came. Meanwhile, we waited. We waited under duress; we wanted them to come, and we wanted them to leave as swiftly as possible. We needed to lift the heavy burden of fear that had settled on us.

During earlier deportations, Rumkowski ordered the Jewish ghetto police or the Jewish ghetto *Sonder,* "special force," to be in charge; at times, however, he deployed both of them. These men were not as brutal as the Germans—they "simply" followed orders, and rounded up everyone whose name appeared on their list. *Did they have a choice? Were they as helpless as the rest of us?* Questions such as these ran through my mind as we, who waited for we-knew-not-what, were jolted by harsh, gutteral sounds, and a clamor. The Germans had arrived! They carried rifles, held onto the leashes of vicious, barking dogs, and were in wait at the wheels of huge, as-yet-empty trucks. They went from building to building, from room to room.

The Germans shouted: *"Raus. Everyone out,"* and we scrambled into the courtyard; we lined up along the fence, and they searched for hidden persons from the attic to the basement. When they found several older people, they beat them mercilessly, and chased them onto the waiting trucks. After this demonstration, they "inspected" us. One at a time, we were processed: *"You to the right; you to the left."* Scarcely realizing what had happened, Karin and I were no longer together. She had been pushed onto a truck, along with more than half of the tenants in our building—and Dorka was among them. I caught sight of Karin as her hands reached out to me, but the drawn rifles of the Germans threatened and barred me from approaching her. Seconds later the truck sped away. I never saw her again.

A small remainder of numb, silent beings stood in the courtyard. Every room in every apartment of the building had lost several occupants. Fathers and mothers, grandfathers and grandmothers, and all the young boys and girls had been taken. None in the critical categories had been able to elude the Germans and suddenly, our wails burst into the still air. My soul was wrenched, and cried for Karin: *Where are they taking you? Will I see you again?* In shock, I dragged myself to my room. This time, it was uncrowded and eerily quiet. Mrs. Heilbronn and I were the only ones to have returned.

When the curfew was lifted on September 12th, we were ordered back to work. Thousands upon thousands of Jews had been taken away by the Germans, and we now awaited news from those we were destined never to hear from again.

After the debacle, we once more collected our meager food rations—and on the surface, it seemed that life had settled back into the usual routine. Those of us who were still in the ghetto continued to decline. We were weak and demoralized.

I had been raised as an Orthodox Jew, and had been taught that there is a God in whose mercy I can trust—but in my forsaken state, I began to doubt. My parents had been murdered, Karin and Dorka were gone, and my unhappy friend, Bronia, no longer came to see me. A week after the deportations I learned that Bronia had hidden in the offices at Balucki Rynek; a passing German had seen and grabbed her and thrown her onto a truck. She was gone. My nights were now filled with the voices and faces of the past, and the thought that one day the Germans would get me, too.

Rumkowski now concentrated on the efficiency of the factories; he insisted on daily quotas and an ever-increasing output to satisfy the Germans' demands. We were manufacturing anything and everything from ladies' hats and corsets to braided rugs, furniture, army boots, etc.—and all of these goods were shipped to the Reich for German consumption. Meanwhile, at every opportunity, Rumkowski preached: *"Unser einziger Weg ist Arbeit."* Our only way is work. Was it possible that Rumkowski honestly believed the Germans would let us live, as long as we worked until we dropped?

© Zydowski Instytut Historyczny, Warsaw

*Children deported from Lodz Ghetto, 1942*

*"The Only Way is Work!"*
*Sign on a Lodz Ghetto wall*

# 4

## ᴥ Privation and Privilege ᴥ

IN THE FALL OF 1942, AS A RESULT OF ONE OF RUMKOW-
ski's whims, I found myself out of a job. On an impulse
Rumkowski had decided that our office was "nonessen-
tial" and had shut it down. Forty workers were cast out,
and we had to hustle for new jobs—or actually, any kind
of work—in order to qualify for the daily noontime bowl
of soup.

I was among the fortunate ones. Szaja Spiegel and
Henryk Neftalin, who were in charge of the third-floor
offices, hired me to work on records pertaining to the
allocation of coal for various German cities. Certain
forms were sent into the ghetto, for us to fill in and complete, that were then returned to the Reich. My new assignment allowed me to work in the same building on
Rybna 8, and for that at least I was glad.

My boss, Henryk Neftalin, was in charge of the entire
project. He was a slim man of medium height; his eyes
and hair were dark, and many would have considered
him good looking were it not for his large, beaked nose.
Winter and summer, rain or shine, it was his idiosyncracy
to wear rubber overshoes and a long, gray scarf wrapped
twice around his neck, and these became his trademark.

Neftalin was an efficient, compassionate, and fair-
minded attorney who was said to have Rumkowski's ear.

He was apparently one of a handful of people whom Rumkowski seemed to respect, although no one really understood why this was so. In his mid-thirties, he was energetic and outspoken. Due to his efforts many ghetto projects were initiated, including the work we did in our office, as well as in the Statistical Department, the Archives—on Plac Koscielny 4—and in many other divisions of labor.

Neftalin's immediate assistant and friend was Szaja Spiegel, who had been a teacher, writer, and poet. He detested working in an office, but, like us all, he needed the daily bowl of soup to help him survive. Szaja too was in his thirties, but he looked older: he was stocky and rarely smiled, characteristically slow and deliberate in action, and forever preoccupied with writing. Everyone liked or even admired him and his works—everyone, that is, but Rumkowski—but Szaja had no love for Rumkowski either. *"Watch out! Don't fall into Rumkowski's hands,"* he warned. *"He is a rotten human being, a pig!"* Szaja, who repeated these and similar remarks frequently, did not bother to elaborate.

Going to work was almost like coming home. My job was interesting from time to time, and my coworkers were kind and friendly—but I liked Szaja best, because he paid attention to me. Within weeks we were friends, and within months we were very much in love—but the ghetto was hardly the ideal place for lovers. There were no flowers or exchange of gifts for courtship and, more importantly, there was little or no hope—other than the dubious prospect of a life "after the war."

On a dark, cloudy day in January of 1943, Rumkowski dropped in on Henryk Neftalin unexpectedly. He was not very happy. "You have too many people who sit behind their desks," he said. "I need them to work in the metal shop and straw-shoe factory. Your people have to contribute more. Here, in the ghetto, we are all equal." Changes were about to take place.

Rumkowski had asserted that we were "equal" many times before, but we understood the meaning of the word better than he—for our only equality rested in the rites of universal suffering and starvation. Did we matter to the Germans or anyone else? No. We were Jews. None seemed to care whether we lived or died, and some obviously preferred the latter.

Room by room, office workers were asked to line up and appear before Rumkowski. He talked to some and he joked with others; he scolded now this one, now that one—and, in the end, he directed more than half of us to the factories. I had hidden, but I made sure I could see everything through an open door. Several hours later, Henryk Neftalin's secretary walked into the hallway. She carried a piece of paper from which she read off the names of the five or six people who, like me, had not come forward, and we were escorted to Neftalin's office.

Rumkowski sat in the middle of the room, his right hand resting on his cane. His hat and coat were off—and, for the first time, I could really *see* him. My first impression was that he stooped and was not as tall as I had thought; then I noted that his hair was white and sparse, he was clean-shaven, and he peered through his black-rimmed glasses. Thoughts about Bronia and what she had told me ran through my mind as I observed him— but when I looked at the knee-length, highly polished black boots he wore, I saw that they were identical to those worn by the Gestapo, and I shivered.

Against the wall stood Henryk Neftalin, Szaja Spiegel,

Aaron Jakubowicz, Bernard Fuchs, and several other ghetto dignitaries I could not identify. To me they appeared to be a composition straight out of a fairy tale, a picture of a king on a throne, scepter in hand, surrounded by courtiers; we, of course, were the peasants awaiting the pronouncements ... For a split second something almost laughable had occurred to me, but I soon returned to the reality of the moment and the seriousness of the occasion.

The first person to step forward was a young woman, plainly dressed, with short, brown hair. "Your name?" Rumkowski wanted to know. She replied in a barely audible whisper, and Rumkowski stared at her for a few moments. Then he said: "As of tomorrow, you will work in the straw-shoe factory." The secretary, who took notes, dismissed her: "You may leave. *Next!*"

In due course, another two women stepped forward. The procedure for each was identical and, with his left hand, Rumkowski both dismissed and waved them on. The fourth woman gave her name as "Luba," and I recognized her at once. She was the same person with whom I had bartered an alligator purse for two wedges of bread a little more than a year earlier. She looked older now and wore a great deal of makeup—but she was well dressed, and would have seemed confident were it not for the sadness in her eyes when she smiled. Rumkowski evidently knew her, for she was quite at ease when she spoke to him. They whispered to one another and laughed; then he kissed her cheek—and she stayed. Why, I wondered, had she received such special treatment?

Someone tapped me on the shoulder. I jumped out of fear, and the secretary pushed me forward. I now stood before Rumkowski, and dared not breathe. I was terrified—but Rumkowski reached for my hand, and spoke to me in Yiddish: "Your name? Where do you come from? Do you have a family?"

I replied like an automaton:

"Cecilia Landau. The Germans sent me to the ghetto from Hamburg in October 1941. My parents are dead, and my sister was deported. I have no one . . ." My Yiddish sounded rather German, and he smiled at me. "Little German, you will hear from me! Meanwhile, go back to work." He released my hand and I murmured, "Thank you," before rushing out of the room. At my desk, I heaved a sigh of relief. I had passed "inspection."

The following week Henryk called Luba and me into his office. "You two are to be transferred to the Statistical Archives. From now on you will work for Dr. Oskar Singer at Plac Koscielny 4, where you will be safer." Neftalin did not explain, and I wondered what he meant.

Luba and I were assigned to type Dr. Singer's notes, keep his records, and do the filing. The office itself was large and unheated, and we had to wear our coats and gloves at all times; sometimes we even had to walk back and forth in order to keep from freezing. We worked side by side and I soon learned that Luba was actually vivacious; she had an infectious laugh and was very outspoken. As it happened, she did not recognize me—and for some strange reason, I thought it best to say nothing.

The two of us were together ten hours a day. Two or three of those hours were spent in transcribing Dr. Singer's notes and filing them. After that, we waited for him to return to the office. Most of his days were spent "on the street"—as he used to say—but we knew that he visited various dignitaries in order to get an occasional food coupon or additional information on ghetto "hap-

© Jüdisches Museum, Frankfurt

*Plac Kościelny, Lodz Ghetto*
(*Celia worked in the building at the far left*)

penings." Since Luba and I had little or nothing to do much of the time, we exchanged stories, dreamed of food, and spoke of our hunger. *Food, food, food!* It was always on our minds as we visualized limitless slices of bread, and the huge party we would have after the war.

Luba shared information with me without inhibition, but I hesitated to confide in her. I was now at least a half-hour's walk away from the old office, and I missed Szaja. I thought of him often, but we could only meet at night—he waited for me every evening after work. Once together, we walked arm in arm to the dismal room that was the only home I had.

*"I will remove the troublemakers in the workshops!"* Rumkowski's latest slogan blared out at us. Unrest beset the factories; strikes were threatened and demands were made for more food, but none of it amounted to anything. In the end, both the Germans in Lodz and the Jews

in the ghetto came to feel that maybe, *just maybe*, Rumkowski could succeed in convincing Berlin that *his* Jews were needed for the war effort, and that they had to have more food.

Rumkowski was temperamental, unpredictable, narcissistic, quick to anger, and vengeful. When displeased—and that was often—his rage demonstrated the confidence he placed in his authority over us. He was disliked and hated by the many, and envied by the few. He had enough food as the absolute ruler of the ghetto, and he had unquestionable skills as an organizer. He alone kept the factories busy, and he alone was responsible for pressuring us to produce greater quantities of goods for the Germans. Among ourselves we asked: "Is Rumkowski with us, or with the Germans?"

During the turbulence, Luba was as irrepressible as ever—and I had to listen to her running comments for hours on end. One day, when I finally asked her to tell me about herself and her life, it was all the encouragement she needed. She pulled her chair close to mine, and began at once:

"I grew up in the orphanage at Helenowek, and lived there from the time I was quite young until I was about seventeen. I have never been able to remember anything about my parents, but I do know that they died when I was very young. Many years ago I used to look at several of the faded photographs I had of them—but after a while, I stopped. I could not retrieve a single memory. I have no other relatives, and so I had no choice other than to accept my fate. Just before the war, I was old enough to do kitchen work: I mopped floors and washed dishes, and always made sure that no one saw my tears or suspected my unhappiness. I looked forward to the day when I would be old enough to leave—like so many others before me—but I often wondered if they were happier away from Helenowek.

"It was at Helenowek that I met Rumkowski. He was in charge of the orphanage, and came around often. From the very beginning of my stay, he established the practice of calling me into his office and locking the door after me. When I was trapped like that, he undressed me and did terrible things to me. I cried in revulsion and rage; I begged and pleaded, to no avail. Rumkowski did not stop. I hated the sight of him and his touch, but I hated myself more for not putting an end to his despicable behavior. I was being violated, but I was and always have been practical. I knew there was nothing I could have done.

"Just once, shortly before the war began, a man by the name of Sergei came to the orphanage to interview some of us who had been molested. I told him the truth, and he promised that things would change—but the war broke out, and no action was taken. When I came to the ghetto, I found that Rumkowski had been appointed by the Germans to head the *Judenrat*."

When I asked, "Did you go back to the orphanage?" Luba laughed at me. The laugh was harsh and metallic—decidedly strange for one so young.

"*Are you crazy?* I found a room, which had been partitioned off from a larger one on Zgierska Street. It is just large enough for a bed and a chair, and my clothes hang on the nails I hammered into the wall. I keep one bucket with clean water in it in a corner of the room—which I bring up from the pump downstairs—and another bucket in the room for the slop. I empty that one by flushing it into the open gutter."

She took a deep breath, and went on:

"Work was difficult to come by, and for months I looked for a job without success. Finally, I found something in the metal factory. It was hard work, but I got my noonday soup. Eventually, I ended up in the offices on Rybna 8, but that's another story."

For several days after our exchange Luba did not say much, and she did not attempt to continue her story. Then, one day, she surprised me by asking:

"Did I tell you about Genek?"

"No, you didn't."

"I usually get my food rations at the distribution center on Lutomierska Street," she began. "When I first went there, I immediately noticed the manager. The poster on the wall listed his name as *Genek*. He was about forty, tall, blond, and very good looking. I made sure to wear make-up, and to dress well whenever I went there; I wanted Genek to notice me, and it was not long before he did. One day as I stood in line, he slowly made his way through the queue and came straight up to me. He took my ration cards away—as well as the bag I had brought along with me, which was filled with containers for the various food items—and then he motioned for me to wait by the wall. Not a word had been spoken. Those who saw him yelled: '*Not fair! She has to wait her turn, like the rest of us!*' Genek, however, had already disappeared behind the counter. He instructed a woman to fill my containers, and she weighed each item carefully before doing so. After that, she put everything in my shopping bag. Genek then took the bag, walked toward the door, and this time he motioned for me to follow him. I was speechless. He had helped me by singling me out, and he obviously had influence. I was pleased—but before I could thank him, he handed me the bag and asked: 'How about a walk tonight? Let's say around seven, when I get off work?' I was delighted. 'Of course, that will be fine. I live at number 24 Zgierska Street, and will wait for you downstairs.' Without speaking again, Genek turned and walked away.

"I spent that entire afternoon getting ready. I chose a sweater and skirt from my limited wardrobe, and decided that my old, threadbare coat would have to do despite the cold. I combed my hair, applied makeup, and then removed and applied it again. I was nervous and excited. For the first time, I forgot the food and did not eat. Precisely at seven I was downstairs, waiting for Genek. He was not there—and I worried that he would not come at all—but twenty minutes later, he appeared. He smiled, without apologizing for the delay. *Honestly, I didn't care!* He had come, and I was happy!"

Luba inhaled deeply, made sure I was attentive, and went on: "We walked through the streets of the ghetto for about two hours, carefully avoiding the barbed wire and guardhouses. I definitely wanted to know more about him, so I asked: 'How did you get a job in the food distribution center?' He smiled, said that it helped to know influential people, and laughed.

"Genek's words and what they implied impressed me, and I wasted no time in letting him know what I wanted. I told him that I worked in the metal factory, and that the work was dirty and difficult; after that, I asked him if one of his 'friends' could help me get another job. I told him that I would be very grateful, and that I knew how to show my appreciation. He seemed surprised at how direct I was—but I felt my honesty had reached him, for he replied by saying: 'I will look into it tomorrow. Come to the store in a day or two, and I will let you know what I learn.'

"It had gotten dark, and we should have paid attention to the curfew. The sky was clear—but the frost had settled on our coats, and our breath left steamy clouds in the air. It was too cold and dangerous to stay out any longer, and Genek led me home again. At the door he grabbed hold of me and kissed me for what seemed like a long time. My first reaction was one of shock—but later on I realized his attention pleased me. Never before did I have a date, and no one had ever kissed me.

"Without warning, Genek pushed me away from him, and asked: 'Do you live alone?' He had pried, and I was embarrassed by the question, so I said '*No*,' and bid him a hasty good night. I went to my room and undressed, but I could not sleep. I dreamed of marriage and a future with Genek—an entirely new life—once the war is over."

While Luba paused and remained quiet, I thought of how I may have prejudged her. She had given me the impression that she was a tough, ruthless, and opportunistic person, but I found my attitude softening. She had been an orphan for as long as she could remember, and she certainly deserved a happier life—but even as I began to understand and sympathize, I wondered why I continued to feel uncomfortable when I was with her.

It was now quite late, and the time had come to close the office. Luba and I shook hands in parting and made our way to our rooms—which were in opposite directions. The next few days we were busy with work, so almost a week went by before she could continue:

"I did not hear from Genek as he had promised, and I finally decided to walk to the food store. When I got there, I found him in his office. He seemed pleased to see me, and once again offered no apology for not having gotten in touch with me. He sat where he was and smiled. 'I have good news for you,' he said. 'Go to the offices at Rybna 8, and ask for Lola Klein. I told her to expect you.'

"I followed Genek's advice and asked for Lola Klein. Someone directed me to a small room where a woman in her mid-thirties sat behind a desk. She was a blonde who wore glasses, and she did not pay the slightest attention to me when I said 'Good morning.' Finally, I said: 'Excuse me. Genek Kaminsky told me that he had spoken to you, and that you might have a job for me.' She raised her eyes, and scrutinized me for a long time. I was no competition for her but, nevertheless, she asked: 'Do you know Genek Kaminsky well?' 'No, I do not. I just pick up my rations at his store.'

"Lola seemed satisfied with my reply, and told me: 'I will give you a clerical job in Section I. Report for work early tomorrow morning.' I was delighted, and said: 'Thank you. I will do a good job,' but she had nothing more to add. She went back to studying the stack of papers on her desk—and, when she did not look up again, I turned around and walked out.

"The following morning, I reported for work. I found that the job was boring, but I got soup at noon—a watery mess of cabbage leaves and a small potato. It was tasteless, but it was fairly warm, and filled my stomach. I would have loved to have had more food, but there was none. On the way home that night, I went to see Genek. I said: 'Thank you for the job; I am grateful, and appreciate your help,' and then I asked him if we could take a walk. He looked at me for a while and seemed to be thinking; finally he replied: 'Okay. I will be there at seven.'

"I rushed home, washed, changed my clothes, and waited. He was late, but he had come! Once more, I was happy to see him. We talked about my work at the office, the crowds at the food distribution center, and whether or not the next allotment would contain sugar or margarine. It was terribly cold; the icy wind blew through our coats, and before long Genek turned around and dropped me off at the front door. He kissed me—and then complained: 'Meeting like this is useless. We will have to get you a place of your own. I want to be able to visit.'

"I was afraid of losing him and nodded in agreement, but I was not convinced this was the right thing to do. He appeared to be a distant, secretive man, who shared little of his life—but he knew everyone of importance and was very sure of himself. He seemed to be the sort of person whose every wish or whim is granted—and I was aware of this—but I could not help myself. I did not want to be alone, and I wanted Genek."

As I listened to her, I realized how cold and calculating she could be. Love was not involved; she simply took advantage of circumstances to serve her own interests. I had never met anyone quite like her, and I pitied her. I did not admire the crudity of her behavior, but I marveled at how well she coped.

The following day, Luba went on: "Genek started picking me up frequently. Our walks became shorter—our good-byes and kisses in the hallway, longer. For the first time I was happy. I had a job, the additonal soup—and above all, Genek.

"One night when I returned to my room, I found Genek seated on my bed. He had brought two carpenters along with him, and had transformed the room with several pieces of plywood. My roommates now had a larger area for themselves, while a small hallway had been partitioned off and made into a tiny nest for me. I had enough space for my bed and a stove, a table and a chair. You can imagine how surprised I was. Genek had never mention-ed his intention to partition the room, and had made all the decisions without my knowledge. He had taken me for granted. I dared not object—however, I felt that I needed an immediate answer to the question of whether or not he would marry me.

"Genek was perplexed, but he replied without hesita-tion. '*No*. Marriage is out of question. *Suit yourself*. If you like, I won't come back.' He was cold and distant, and I was frightened. *Lose Genek? Give him up, and be alone again?* I had nothing to say. He had made his position clear, and I felt I had no choice other than to submit.

"The carpenters left as soon as Genek 'paid them' with several slices of unwrapped, crumbled, stale bread, which he had pulled out of his jacket pocket. He now looked happy, smiled, and motioned for me to sit next to him on the bed. We kissed for a long time. Not a word was spoken as he undressed me gradually, and made love to me.

"My feelings were in a state of turmoil and I closed my eyes—but when Genek touched me, I saw Rumkow-ski's face. I saw Rumkowski's piercing eyes behind thick lenses; I saw his lips, and I remembered his impotence over the years. The horror of this memory made me shiv-er as I tried to shake off the past, but it was no use. When I finally opened my eyes, I looked at Genek. He had rolled over onto his side, and had fallen asleep. I had had no pleasure. I feared pregnancy. I had heard of abortions taking place in the ghetto, but I knew they were risky. I knew that a young woman had died of complications only a few months earlier!"

Luba sighed. She looked unhappy. I reached for her

hand and said: "Why don't we continue our talk tomor-row?" I was exhausted and hungry, and I had heard the sound of voices coming our way. Our boss was about to return.

Dr. Singer brought copious notes for us to work on, and sank into a chair. As usual, his notes contained a re-cord of the daily events in the ghetto. These included the rationing and distribution of food, the number of deaths due to starvation or other causes, the suicides and depor-tations, and other statistical data.

"I saw Wolkowna today, and we had a long talk; from there I went to see Dora Fuchs, but she kept me waiting and was not in a talkative mood," said Dr. Singer, who was obviously "in need of talk." He mentioned the young woman in charge of the mattress factory, as well as the director of one of the kitchens, etc., and before long I was struck by the fact that everyone he had spoken of was a woman in a position of responsibility. Up until 1942 women had not held posts of importance, but now, for the first time—even here in the ghetto—women were put-ting their abilities to work and were competing with men. I recalled the past and the times when I had asked one of these "important women" for a job, only to be met with contempt. They were obliging to men, tough and un-yielding to women, and constantly engaged in the strug-gle to retain their positions. Still, I admired them for forging ahead.

The following afternoon, Luba brought a chair to my desk and continued her by-now ritualistic storytelling:

"After that first time together, Genek returned for three successive nights. There was very little conversation between us. I wondered about his life—aside from work—and I asked questions, but he was evasive. For four or five evenings he did not show up, and he did not send word. I worried, cried myself to sleep, and finally decided to stop by the food store—but he was not there. When I returned to my room after that day's work, I found that Genek was there, waiting for me. 'Where have you been?' I cried. 'I was beside myself with worry, and didn't know what to do! I heard that you have a mother and sister in the ghetto, but I don't know how to reach them!'

"Genek listened without emotion. 'You will have to get used to the fact that I will not be coming to see you every evening. I will come when I can, and *if* I want to. My family is none of your business, and I don't want you to contact them.' I was surprised and hurt by his anger, and started to cry.

"*I can't make him out at all.* I realize that he takes food from the store and uses it for his own purposes, but I am hungry and he never shares any of the food with me. I am a practical person; my relationship with Genek is based on practicality!"

During the summer of 1943, Rumkowki was seen frequently as he rode through the ghetto. He was dressed in a light overcoat with a matching cap, and he wore the shining, black leather boots we all recognized as those of the Gestapo's—and Luba began speaking of him again:

"I cannot help but admire Rumkowski's new horse-drawn carriage, well-fed horse, and equally well-fed driver, but I remember how he hissed and hurled angry words at me when I tried to repel his advances. I was a powerless child in an orphan asylum then—but to this day he frightens me with the threats he makes to keep me from reporting him. His power pervades the ghetto and seems limitlesss when I hear him threaten deportation, or learn of how he either imprisons Jews for minor offenses or turns them over to the Germans. I know that he asked the Gestapo to deport Diana Szajn from the ghetto and that the Germans took her away. She was never heard from again, and we don't know where she is.

"I shudder when I think of him, but I know that he doles out favors. Sometimes it is food; sometimes it is a job. *He even performs marriages, as if he were a rabbi!* I am tempted to ask him for extra food or a better job—maybe one in a bakery—but I know I will have to pay, and I am determined to stay away from him."

For several days Luba did not talk to me. She was quiet and seemed disturbed. When I asked what troubled her, she looked at me for a long time before answering:

"Genek found out that I knew Rumkowski before the war, and began to pester me to go to him in order to ask for bread and other foods. I told him I did not want to do this, but he said that if I did not go, it meant I did not love him. I could not tell him I refused to see Rumkowski because I knew he would abuse me. In the end, though, I capitulated. I felt I had no choice, and I gave in. I waited for the approach of Rumkowski's carriage at the entrance to Balucki Rynek and, when it appeared, I stepped into its path. The carriage stopped short, and I addressed Rumkowski: 'Mr. President, do you remember me? I am in need of your help, please . . .' He smiled, nodded, and said that I could see him in his office any day after four. I went to him reluctantly. My name was already on a list, and the guard let me pass.

"Rumkowski sat behind his desk, and asked: 'What do you want, my child?' My God, his tone was pleasant!

"'Please, Mr. President,' I replied: 'Let me have a coupon for bread. I am terribly hungry.' Rumkowski got up and walked over to where I stood: he looked at me, made sure the door was locked, and began to undress me. I will spare you the disgusting details of what happened next, but perhaps you can imagine what I went through . . ."

"Did you get the food coupon?"

"Yes, I did. I confronted him and said: 'Mr. President I want the *coupons* now.' At the time Rumkowski was surprised by my brashness, but he has gotten used to it—and now, he always hands over several coupons for bread, sugar, and sometimes even margarine.

"I hate the person I have become, but Genek was delighted to see the food. He, in fact, made plans for me to return immediately so I could ask for more. I delayed as long as I could, but Genek persisted—and, like a fool, I went again. I returned to Rumkowski and always got what I came for, but I had to endure his groping, molesting hands. I can tell you in all honesty that I have never hated anyone as much as I hate this man!"

There was nothing I could say, and I never mentioned the incident again.

Luba was moody; she was her usual, lively self one minute and depressed and withdrawn the next. When she came into the office one morning, her face was streaked in tears. "Genek has been arrested. He is in the ghetto jail, and I don't know why. I went to see him, and was finally allowed to visit. He pleaded with me to urge Rumkowski to release him. The rumor is that Genek was caught stealing food from the store, and if this is true, it is a very serious crime.

"I went to see Rumkowski—and, after much pleading and many tears, he finally agreed to release Genek. From now on Genek will no longer be able to work in the ghetto, and I will have to go to Rumkowski whenever he sends for me."

I should have been stunned, but much of what I had learned did not come as a surprise. I remembered how Genek had provided two wedges of bread for my alligator purse, and reasoned that he must have stolen much more than that.

A few days later, Luba interrupted my thoughts with a further report: "Genek is out of jail. His friends have him registered in the rug factory and, once a day, he goes there to pick up his soup. It is illegal to do this, and I can only hope that no one reports him.

"He comes to my room and stays the night, but there is never any talk or expression of love. I feel his only interest is in sex, and I am angry. I hate sex, and I hate all men; there is no thrill, no joy, no love!"

For days on end the once-happy, chatty Luba remained quiet. We sat in the same office and shared the work to be done, but neither of us had anything to say. One day during the following week, Luba came in late. We were supposed to be at our desks at eight, but it was just about ten when she arrived. Her face was tear stained again and white as chalk. She walked slowly, as if in pain, held onto the walls, and sank to the floor, moaning involuntarily.

"Luba, what's wrong? Shall I get help?"

"*No!*" she screamed, and then she sprawled across the floor, raising her legs to her chest in a near-fetal position, and lay there inconsolably. I rolled her jacket up and placed it under her head. I was frantic and helpless; Luba cried and moaned. Finally, I pleaded: "Please, please tell me what is wrong!" At last, the words she had so much trouble saying erupted: "I was pregnant . . . Genek insisted on an abortion. He insisted, and then he complained: '*We will have to pay with our bread ration!*'

"Genek came with me as far as the doctor's office, dropped me off at the door, and walked away. I told the doctor I was pregnant, and his response was: '*Can you pay?*' I took a week's bread ration out of my bag and placed it before him, but he only nodded. 'Get undressed; put the robe on, and lie on the table,' he ordered emphatically. I followed his instructions—but the robe was stained with blood, and I began to cry. 'Enough of that,' he shouted. 'I have smelling salts, but I don't have a proper anesthetic. It's a fast and simple procedure, but you have to be quiet. This is illegal!'

"I pressed the smelling salts to my nose, crammed a part of the robe into my mouth, and endured unbelievable pain. The room reeled; I thought of death, and fainted. When I came to, the procedure was done; I was bleeding, and the doctor allowed me to rest for ten minutes. After that, he ordered me to dress and leave. He gave me a few rags with which to absorb the flow of blood, and then I dressed. I felt woozy, but I somehow managed to walk to the office."

The side of Luba's skirt was spotted with blood. My thoughts raced: *What am I to do? Will she die?* I found a large scarf in her purse, folded it, and placed it between her legs; I wiped her forehead, watched her closely, and prayed that Dr. Singer would not return. Two hours later, Luba seemed calmer—and I hoped the pain had eased. When she finally fell asleep, I began to cry. I was furious with Genek for getting her pregnant and insisting on an abortion, and I hated him for his callousness in leaving her so alone.

That day we were in luck. Dr. Singer had not returned, and by late afternoon I urged Luba to sit up and clean her face. "Put your coat on. We'll walk to your room together. You can't stay here," I said, and Luba nodded in agreement. I helped her, and we somehow managed to walk down the stairs, out of the building, and through the crowded streets. When we got to her room, I took the key out of her alligator purse and opened the door. Luba collapsed on the bed and motioned for me to leave. She was afraid that Genek would be angry to see me there. "Please hurry," she cried, and I walked out.

The following morning, an ashen-faced Luba was back at work. "Genek came to see me last night. 'Don't be a fool,' he scolded. 'There is no way you can keep a baby in the ghetto!' He sounded cruel and ugly, and I feel no love for him."

In the days that followed, Luba gradually grew stronger. Never once did she refer to the abortion, or what it had revealed about Genek's character. Meanwhile, I too remained silent.

Monday morning, a telephone call for our office came from the adjacent office, a common enough occurrence, since neither we nor most of the offices in the ghetto had telephones. Chawa, who worked next door, ran into our room to say: "Rumkowski's office called. Both of you are to see him there tomorrow morning. There may be a job for you in the newly formed workers' kitchen." She was excited, but the news caught us by surprise. We had had no idea that Rumkowski might be thinking along these lines. Tuesday morning we informed Dr. Singer of our appointment with Rumkowski, and he smiled. His daughter Elli and about forty others, all young women, had been summoned too.

The room on Balucki Rynek was crowded with the young women who had been told to report, and Rumkowski spoke briefly: "You have been selected to work in one of three evening kitchens. Mr. Mintz will assign you to your location. For two weeks only, a deserving worker will come to the kitchen and receive an evening meal. After two weeks, a new group of workers will be selected for the next fourteen days, and so on." There was applause and laughter, after which Mr. Mintz proceeded to give us our assignments. Luba and I were sent to Mlinarska Street. She was to work as a waitress; I was to work in the office, keeping track of the provisions we used in the kitchen.

When we returned to the Department of Statistical Archives, Dr. Singer was pleased for us. Szaja, however, became agitated, and warned: "Be careful. Rumkowski is dangerous." As usual, he cautioned me without offering any explanation. Little did he realize how much I had been learning about Rumkowski. At eighteen, I was sure I could handle any situation!

*These Are My Five Mottoes:*
*1. Bread, 2. Work, 3.Care for the Sick, 4. Care for the Children,*
*5. Peace within the Ghetto.*

5

## ✦ *Ominous Words from a Dead Soul* ✦

THE FALL OF 1943 WAS LARGELY OVERCAST, AND MY thoughts were gloomy. Blue, clear skies seemed to be deserting us, and only rarely did the sun break through the clouds to warm our emaciated bodies. The young and the old were dying of starvation, and sporadic deportations continued to take their toll. Those *selected* for "resettlement" were fewer in number than in the past, but many did not want to leave for the unknown. In our predicament, however, one's wishes were of little or no account. The person whose name appeared on a list had no choice, and was generally defenseless unless a Zionist, Bundist, Communist, or other comrade with connections looked out for his interests in an act of solidarity. In such cases, the unfortunate and bitter reality substituted one human for another. Specific individuals were not of interest to the Germans, but rather the *number of Jews* required to satisfy the quota for a given transport in a chain of deportations. Those who remained for the time being continued to live a day at a time; we were "temporary," anxious, and hungry, and often ill with typhus and other ailments.

In spite of our gnawing hunger and depressed state, activities at the evening kitchen operated at a feverish pace. We worked hard to get everything ready—from dishes to pots and pans, tables and chairs—but most importantly, we saw that the allocated provisions were delivered to the cooks so the hungry could eat.

Generally, we served a small patty of meat—no one spoke about the fact that it was horsemeat—a spoonful of either beets, turnips, or carrots, and a few slivers of potato or another vegetable. Potato peels were saved in large bags, and these were distributed to those who were fortunate enough to have obtained a special coupon. We had sunk very low to have now begun to vie for the precious potato peels!

The storeroom, which contained sacks of flour, sugar, and other staples, was carefully guarded by Salka Meyerowicz—a small, dark-haired young woman about whom it was rumored that her father knew Rumkowski before the war. Key in hand, she permitted no one to step over the threshhold of her domain. She was scrupulous about locking the door when she worked outside or left for the day, and would not trust anyone. We eyed the provisions longingly—and our aching stomachs contracted—but we were comforted by the promise of a meal. Unfortunately, it was distributed in the late afternoon or early evening, just before the first arrivals came to the kitchen for their meal, and we were quite nervous by that time.

The day the kitchen was inaugurated, we were ready for the streams of people sure to come—but we were rather apprehensive. Rumkowski had announced he would be there for the opening, and a great deal rested upon his approval. Those who served the food were lined up—and three young women sat at the entrance, ready to clip coupons. Meanwhile I sat in a tiny cubicle that served as an office, trying to figure out how many grams of food each person would consume. By this time, I had come to realize that all of us who worked in the kitchen had some sort of connection to Rumkowski. Strangely enough, no one spoke of the past or admitted she knew him. Each girl guarded her "privilege," or *protectectzia*, as it was called—and for some reason beyond my comprehension, this "protection" was not to be acknowledged openly.

At five o'clock we were given the meal we had earned. The dining room fell silent and we wolfed down our food, oblivious to taste. I remember that although I was still hungry, I wrapped the patty in newspaper and stored it in my pocket. Later on, when he came to pick me up, I gave it to Szaja. We had been warned not to do what I had just done—but I saw that others had had the same thought, and that I was not alone.

At six o'clock sharp, the doors of the kitchen were opened. A large crowd surged in, and just about then a *droshki* drove up. The swell of applause and cheers that greeted it left no doubt that Rumkowski had arrived. I left my post at the desk and peered out through a crack in the door. I watched as Rumkowski examined the tables, food, and servers, who stood in a line like soldiers at attention. A young woman had not tied her apron strings neatly enough to suit Rumkowski's taste, and he hit her across the shoulders with his cane. "Be more careful in the future, all of you," he warned. "Your jobs depend on it. I will conduct frequent inspections, and I will come unannounced."

After this pronouncement, Rumkowski turned around and walked toward the storeroom. He pushed Salka Meyerowicz inside, and shut the door. Everyone saw this, and no one said a word.

Troubling thoughts about evildoing raced through

my mind as I returned to my desk, but I could not concentrate. About twenty minutes later, I heard the uneven gait of loud, *dragging* footsteps, and a cane striking the floor at regular intervals. I knew at once that this was Rumkowski's step and, once more, I referred to the worksheets on my desk. I tried to concentrate and do something, but it was hopeless.

Rumkowski entered the office, closed the door behind him, and pulled a chair across the floor. He sat next to me, and I had no choice other than to lift my head. "How are you?" he grinned. "Are you happy to be here?" Over and over again I repeated to myself: *Just answer politely and carefully, and don't upset the man.* Above all, I had to appear steady. "I am pleased with the work and the evening meal. It means a great deal to me, and I thank you," I said. Somehow, I had succeeded in affecting outward calm.

Rumkowski placed his arm around my shoulder, bent toward me, and kissed me on the cheek. "Are you *really* grateful for what I have done for you?" I nodded. "*Tell me,* do you have family abroad?"

"I have two uncles, and several cousins who live in Palestine."

"Those uncles? Are you close to them?"

"Yes. We were in contact before the war."

"One day the war will end. Will you go to Palestine?"

"Yes. I hope so."

"When the war ends, your uncles will have to help me. I want you to promise that you will ask them to do so, and that you will never forget what I have done for you. *"You must always remember how much you owe me for feeding you."*

My calm dissipated; I was in terror, and could only

nod. *"That is not enough,"* Rumkowski hissed. *"I want to hear your promise, now!"* "I promise to ask my uncles in Palestine to help you after the war."

I had replied cautiously, and Rumkowski seemed satisfied. He kissed me once more, this time on the lips, and I shuddered in disgust as he said: "I'll be back soon. We have much to settle." When he left, I heaved a sigh of relief—but his parting words alarmed me. I was afraid, and I dreaded seeing him again.

Rumkowski did not reappear for several days. During that period, and at a moment when no one else was present, Luba took me by the hand and said: "Listen to me. I am only a little older than you are, but I am wiser and more experienced. You know that before the war I was one of the children Rumkowski abused in the orphanage, and you know that I know him. Be very careful; he is a vile person, and he has an explosive temper. He is all-powerful, and he will intimidate anyone to get what he wants. I am not his only victim; he has a history of using young girls. When he takes them into his office, he does unspeakable, indecent things to them."

Luba's concern startled me. *"And now?"* I asked. Luba collected her thoughts before speaking: "Nothing has changed. To this day, he blackmails his intended victim by innuendo. I *still* have to go to his office ..."

Luba could not go on. Tears streamed down her face. I put my arm around her, and remained silent. *What was there to say?* I was sad for Luba, and worried about myself. *What could I do in the face of such heartbreak and powerlessness? How would this play itself out?* Under other circumstances, I would resist such a man; I would fight back, scream, kick, or run, but these were not ordinary times. It was inconceivable for anyone to challenge Rumkowski; he was a vindictive man and, at the very least, prison or deportation awaited the foolhardy. *Maybe Rumkowski will leave me alone,* I thought; *maybe I am an exception.* I was utterly exhausted, somewhat irrational, and not altogether confident.

I dreaded seeing Rumkowski again, and was grateful for every night that passed without his showing up at the office. On the fourth night after my talk with Luba, however, he arrived amid much fanfare and applause. It seemed that, in the ghetto, only those who waited for their evening meal were happy. Rumkowski scolded a few of the girls, and hit those who displeased him; after that, he made his way to me. My heart skipped a beat as his cane thumped the floor and his heavy, uneven steps drew closer.

Rumkowski entered, slammed the door shut, and swept a chair across the floor. He sat close to me as I tried to inch away, but he clamped onto my shoulder like a vise from which there was no escape. With his free hand he grabbed hold of my hand and, before I knew it, placed it on his penis. He forced me to rub it back and forth and I tried to pull away—but his fingers gripped my hand tightly and his nails dug deeply into my flesh. I was filled with horror, fear, and loathing, and I did not know what to do as he continued to coerce me. Back and forth went my hand, with Rumkowski hoarsely commanding: *"Make it work!"*

I prayed for someone to come into the office—but by now, the kitchen was quite deserted. My mind raced. Even if someone were there, I could not expect help; I knew what had happened in the past; I had seen both silence and denial in action. For twenty minutes or so, I lived a nightmare; they were long, slow minutes, and they seemed like an eternity.

When Rumkowski freed my hand, his first words were: "I think I will get you an apartment adjacent to the kitchen, so that I can visit you at any time." I sobbed and pleaded in shock: "Please, Mr. Chairman, let me stay where I am! I am accustomed to my roommates, and I don't want to move!"

"How dare you refuse me?" he screamed, and hit me across the face. "You will do what I say! No one opposes me!" Within seconds, however, he seemed to regret his outburst. He kissed my lips and face, wiped my tears with a white, fragrant handkerchief, stood up, and pulled me up and away from the chair. He embraced me in a rough manner, and held onto me; he pressed his body close to mine and lewdly rolled back and forth. Finally, he let go. He was through with me, and left.

From then on, the same ordeal was repeated over and over again. Whenever Rumkowski visited the kitchen, he came to the office and forced himself on me. Week upon week, the horror and loathing compounded until—beside myself, and in utter desperation—I confided in Luba. "Don't worry," she laughed. "So far, he has done nothing but 'play around,' disgusting as it may be. He hasn't undressed you, and he hasn't 'fondled' your naked body—but what if he does? Even then, you don't have to worry. He is impotent. He can do nothing to you at all," she smiled.

Luba seemed cynical to me, and I did not think what she said was funny. I knew nothing about sex. I was seventeen when my mother died; I had been sheltered, no one had explained the facts of life to me, and I never dared to ask. My relationship with Szaja, although romantic, had remained "pure" and idealistic. I knew nothing about the essentials of procreation—and, in my ignorance of intercourse and its potential, I worried about pregnancy. *What if Rumkowski orders me to move? What then?* On and on, my crazed mind tormented me. The only consolation I had during this period was that Rumkowski no longer talked about getting me an apartment. This alone had I been spared.

I became emotionally and physically ill. My face and neck turned yellow, a high fever debilitated me, and I vomited frequently. I had no choice other than to stay in bed; I could not walk, and I could not work. Luba visited me faithfully; she brought soup to me, and she took away my key so I wouldn't have to open the door for her whenever she could come.

One day Luba said: "I've told Rumkowski that you are not well. He ordered sugar, margarine, and beets for you, and I will bring them tomorrow. I am sorry, but there is no bread. Rumkowski also ordered Dr. Miller to look in on you." For a moment I was grateful, but I soon lost interest. I was too sick to care; my fever had continued to escalate, and I was burning.

The following day, Luba and Dr. Miller came to see me. The doctor examined me in her presence, and afterward shook his head: "I have no medication for either jaundice or gall bladder problems. Just rest," he said. "Let us hope that you do not have hepatitis." The man had been kind and gentle; he could offer no more than that, and I thanked him for coming.

I had no inkling as to the nature or seriousness of my illness; I only knew I was in a state of apathy and I slept around the clock. Luba came, brought soup, and fed me a few spoonsful; she sat by my bed, held my hand, and comforted me. The days passed, and I was essentially oblivious of time.

On the fourth day, a sudden commotion in the hallway and the clamoring of two men awakened me from my stupor. The men banged and knocked on the door, called me by name, and ordered me to reply and open the door. One of the voices seemed to be that of Rumkowski, but I was engulfed in a haze—too weak to either rise or speak. Apart from that, Luba had locked the door from the outside, and without the key it would have been impossible to open the door.

Seven days later I was still jaundiced, weak, and exhausted, but I dragged myself back to work. On that day and to my misfortune, a very angry Rumkowski barged into the office. "I came to see you, but your door was locked. Didn't you hear me? Why didn't you open?"

"I am sorry, but I did not hear you," I lied. "I had a very high fever, and slept most of the time."

Rumkowski grudgingly accepted my explanation and, without warning, said: "If I can save a hundred Jews in the ghetto, everything will have been worthwhile."

The enormity and monstrosity of Rumkowski's words appalled me. One hundred Jews, and no more! This is what he considered an achievement! Not a thought had been spared for those already deported, and not a thought or concern had been expressed for the tens of thousands of small children he had demanded we hand over to the Germans. They were gone, and would never be seen again.

I was still reeling inwardly when Rumkowski grabbed my hand and placed it between his legs. He pressed on and rubbed back and forth as I prayed for the floor to open wide and swallow me whole. I wanted to scream at the top of my lungs; I wanted to run away, never to return, but I could not do anything of the sort. I was a prisoner, and he a demon who decided over life and death. How could I get away from this perverse, maniacal being?

For the next three weeks, we did not see Rumkowski. Meanwhile, rumors spread throughout the kitchen that our food rations would be cut—and this seemed plausible to us, since provisions were in short supply. We worried about losing the jobs that had earned us an extra meal, and wondered what would happen next. When Rumkowski finally appeared, he was somber as he reported: "The Germans have again reduced our provisions. The kitchen will close as of tomorrow, and all of you will report to the saddlery in the morning. You will be sewing leather goods for the German army."

An eerie silence filled the large hall. The kitchen would be closed; food would not be distributed. We walked out slowly and gathered our belongings without saying a word. Once I returned to my room, however, I considered what had happened something of a miracle. Rumkowski no longer would come to the office and, for the time being, I would be out of his reach. We had become accustomed to the privation in the ghetto, but he was insufferable.

*Working in the Saddlery*

## 6

## ⇥ *Closing the Doors to Compassion* ⇤

AFTER ALMOST FOUR YEARS IN THE GHETTO, I BEGAN to feel that each fall and winter arrived earlier and was harsher than the last. The frost was more piercing, the ice more dangerous, and the hunger more intense. During the winter of 1943–1944, the number of those who froze to death in their rooms soared. The opaque flowers of frost that blanketed our windowpanes and obliterated the outside world from view did not melt, even if the midday sun came out. Beautiful as they were, they could not deflect from our misery and squalor.

Ghetto dwellers were now so desperate they resorted to burning the wooden cots upon which they slept. These cots were the property of the ghetto, and anyone caught destroying them would be punished—but no one seemed to care. Records were sketchy, and it was more important to be a little warmer for a few days than to worry about the consequences.

The work at the saddlery was hard and tiring. We missed the extra meal and suffered terribly from hunger, but we no longer worried about Rumkowski's visits and temperamental outbursts. Since it took me an hour to walk from my room to the factory, I was always tired. The leather strips to be sewn together with heavy twine left my fingers raw and blistered, and they bled frequently when the sharp needles pierced the skin—but it was a job, and I could cling to life.

Luba was aloof and talked to no one, but we knew that she managed to see Rumkowski at Balucki Rynek. Her lunch bag said it all, for it contained extra food, sugar, or margarine, which none of us received. Evidently using Rumkowski for leverage, Luba was able to "convince" Genek to marry. A wedding date was set for some time in August, 1944; and, on the condition that the wedding be performed—an event that never took place due to the fact that the liquidation of the ghetto had already begun—she and Genek received a small, modern flat opposite the saddlery, as well as several food coupons. By way of "appreciation," Luba agreed to visit Rumkowski in his office every two or three weeks in order to "satisfy" him. She no longer seemed to mind, and played the game with Rumkowski—making sure she got as much food as she could so that Genek would not complain. Apparently, Genek took no interest in either why or how she received special treatment, and Luba knew that whenever he returned to her, it was on account of the food. All this she unburdened to me on the rare occasions when no one was around, and I listened without envying or pitying her. By now, our morale had deteriorated, and *"Everyone for himself"* had become the ghetto motto ...

After three ghetto winters, the soles of my boots had large holes in them, so that when water or snow seeped in, my toes—which were frostbitten—became irritated. The situation was so serious that I began to worry about whether the frostbite would worsen and lead to gangrene or amputation. These thoughts were, of course, terrifying.

Because my feet felt as heavy as stones and I barely had the strength to drag them along, I decided to embark upon a dangerous course. I would risk imprisonment or deportation in order to steal the leather I needed to resole my boots, and I did not hesitate in implementing my plan. Once or twice a week, and never on the same days, I stole two strips of leather. I made sure that I was not observed, and then I stuffed them hurriedly into my boot. On the evenings when I stole the strips, I walked past the inspection personnel and out into the street, relieved that my treasure had remained hidden and secure. My heart pounded wildly each step of the way, but, although it seemed to me everyone could see through my scheme, I persevered. This was not simple—and taken altogether, the thefts were a long, tediously slow process. Each boot had six strips—but in order to bribe the cobbler to not denounce me, I had to steal an additional twelve strips for him. Using my technique, it therefore took me weeks to complete the theft.

One night as Luba and I were parting, I told her what I had done. She stopped in her tracks, turned white, and cried: "Are you crazy? What if you had been caught?" I shrugged my shoulders. I knew that what I had done was wrong, but ghetto life had made me a thief, and I felt no remorse. All my life I had been taught that decent people do not steal, but I was no longer a decent person. The ghetto had changed me, and it was not a decent place either.

Agony and fear were behind me. The cobbler readily agreed to resole my boots, and greedily looked forward to the twelve strips of leather I would get for him. I was sure that he would not betray me, and that he would probably "buy" a loaf of bread with his prize, but I had learned my lesson. On reflection, I knew that I did not want to be a thief; not here, not anywhere, and I never again stole. My feet were dry once the boots were repaired, but my toes were dark blue and infected.

A sudden calm descended on the ghetto, and un-eventful, hungry days and nights claimed our thoughts during the fall of 1944. Uncertainty was a constant. Hunger pressed us more than ever, food rations were again reduced, and we of the ghetto—apart from being listless and weary—suffered from swollen feet and faces, dysentery and typhus. In four long, hard years the cemetery no longer had space for gravesites, and all the paths along the grounds had to be used in order to bury the dead. In all, more than sixty thousand persons had to be buried there.

After the calm, we were suddenly bombarded by a rash of rumors about a possible move to a labor camp, the approach of the Russian army, and the imminent end of the war—none of which was true at the time. We were incapable of confirming anything, including the impending liquidation of the ghetto. On August 2, 1944, notices were posted everywhere to the effect that entire sections of the ghetto, as well as certain streets, were to be evacuated. Those who were displaced were to report to the rail depot for "resettlement." These were orders, and they were signed by Chaim Rumkowski; they were a far cry from rumors.

The street I lived on was among the first to appear on the list for evacuation, but I had ceased to care; I was tired and emotionally drained. I packed a few belongings, and stored the documents I thought were important enough to take along with me in my father's old, leather briefcase. After that, I locked the door of the room for the last time, and began the long walk toward the wooden bridge to the other side of the ghetto. Believing I had no recourse, I headed for the railroad siding.

*Group Deportations*

© Yad Vashem, Jerusalem

Luba, as it happened, lived on the opposite side of the ghetto—and, for the time being, the evacuation did not affect her. It occurred to me that she and Genek could remain where they were and, on an impulse, I decided to go to their flat. To avoid resettlement at this time, I needed a place to stay, and I was determined to ask for Luba's help until I could work things out.

The walk exhausted me; my belongings dragged me down, and it took me more than two hours to get to Luba's apartment. It was warm and sunny all the way there, so that by the time I climbed the stairs to the second floor, I was in a sweat. I took a breath and knocked; from within, and through the locked door, I heard Luba ask: "Yes? Who is it?"

"I had to leave my room. I have no place to go," I replied. "Please let me come in and rest."

I was met by a silence that surprised me, and I knocked again. This time, Genek's harsh voice barked: "Go away! Don't bother us! We don't want you here!"

Weak and tired, shocked and hurt, and with tears streaming down my face, I turned about and continued to walk to Marysin and the depot. When I arrived, I saw row upon row of mud-spattered, red cattle cars on the tracks. Their gaping doors were narrow, and a wooden ramp led into them. I, along with hundreds of others, lined up; Jewish ghetto police kept order, uniformed Germans stood nearby. Each person received a loaf of bread before mounting the ramp, and then entered the darkness of a hot, crowded cattle car. When my turn came, I saw that a friend named Elli was there with her family— and I did not know whether to be sad or glad. Body against body, we sat on the filthy floorboards, unable to move. The hours passed, and the doors of the cattle car remained open. One woman whimpered occasionally; the old, the young, and one or two small children were paralyzed with fear, and an old man recited the *Shemah*. I broke off a crust of the dry bread we had been given and chewed—but the bread was tasteless, and did nothing to relieve my misery.

By evening, the doors of the cattle car were locked and, amid fitful stops and starts, the train began to move slowly. At the very top of the car was a small opening that was barred from the outside with barbed wire—not a good sign, but at least we had a little air. The hours rolled on. It was impossible to sleep or doze, and we whispered to one another in terror; if we could think at all, we speculated about our destination and what was in store for us. Some of us got ill and used the slop pail in the corner— which was soon filled with a stinking, human waste—but

© Żydowski Instytut Historyczny, Warsaw

*At the railroad station in Marysin,*
*August 1944*

getting to the pail was an ordeal. Mercifully or unmerci-
fully—I do not know which—I was among those who had
no strength to either care for myself or others.

   As the train hesitated through the night and stopped
frequently to let other trains go by, many of which carried
troops, my thoughts turned to the bleak, immediate past.
My father, mother, and sister were gone, and many who
had befriended me had died or been deported. I was sad-

dened by the realization that everyone I loved or cared about had been taken away from me, but when I thought of Rumkowski, I grew ill and angry. To bolster my morale, I tried to picture the future, but somehow I could not imagine it.

By morning, the slits that were strung with barbed wire near the top of the cattle car let in a little air, and the sweltering heat of the day before dissipated. We were now suddenly cold. Some cried; others tried to sleep. We were worn and, more often than not, irritable with one another.

About five in the morning, the train came to a jolting halt. The first of many transports to have signaled the liquidation of the Lodz Ghetto had arrived. From within the car I could hear the shout of the Germans' orders and the barking of dogs. Once the doors were thrown open, I saw a brightly lit platform and the menacing sight of Germans in uniform, holding onto the leashes of restless dogs. *"Raus! Mach schnell! Alles antreten!"* We had to hurry; we had arrived, and we were in Auschwitz. *Things.* They had referred to us as "things," not people—and from this we could infer that our ordeals were not to end, but rather to intensify.

We, who had been the innocent victims of four long years of incarceration in the hermetically sealed ghetto, had never heard of Auschwitz, but we were soon to learn its meaning. Within minutes men were separated from women. Men were marched off, and disappeared into the distance—but women were broken down into two groups: the young and the old. Those who had somehow managed to hide their children from the Germans during the *Sperre,* or those who had children younger than ten, were pulled out and pushed over into the lineup of old women and made to walk along with them. We, who were younger and supposedly fit, were marched off to barracks, ordered to undress, fold our clothes, and remove all jewelry. Our heads and bodies were shaved, and not a strand of hair remained. This was done to immediately identify us as prisoners, as by this time the incoming were arriving in such numbers that the camp personnel could not manage to tattoo each of us with a now-famous Auschwitz identification number. Elli, the friend I had encountered in the cattle car, was so mortified that she timidly asked a nearby *Kapo* if we could be tattooed with a number like hers instead of being shaved, but the *Kapo* laughed coarsely and said: "Here, you take what you get!" Amazingly, the *Kapo* were also Jews, *ka*mp *po*lice chosen from among the prisoners to guard the others. It was a rare prisoner guard who did not treat us as horribly as did the Nazis themselves.

Our hair gone, we were directed to the "showers" at the other end of the barracks. Some of us encountered seasoned prisoners, who tried to prepare us for what might happen. What they said was quite incomprehensible to us, but when we entered the showers we became very agitated. A certain stirring rippled through the chamber; it was whispered from person to person, and it was short and to the point: *gas or water?* When a thin stream trickled over our bodies, we viewed it as a miracle. There was no soap; there were no towels. We were thrown a rag to wear, and nothing more. Shoes and underwear were not for us. After this baffling and humiliating initiation, we were made to march off to other barracks.

That first night in Auschwitz we crowded into narrow cubicles. There were no cots, and we had no straw. In the days to follow, we had to stand at attention for long hours; we were counted over and over again, and received little food. Nothing mattered anymore; the handwriting was on the wall. Auschwitz: the camp of gas chambers, crematoria, and chimneys spewing black, billowing smoke by day and lurid flames by night, left little to the imagination.

In Auschwitz as in Lodz, an active but unreliable rumor mill was in operation. We got word about the many transports that arrived from Lodz and elsewhere; we learned that hundreds of thousands of Jews were involved, and that Rumkowski was among those who had arrived with his family. It was said that Diana Szajn had been waiting for him, and that she had sought him out in order to avenge herself, but it was also said that she had died of typhoid. As for Rumkowski: we heard that he had been murdered within minutes of his arrival—but we also heard that he went to the gas chamber straightaway.

Years of ghetto life had left their mark on me. Whether Rumkowski went directly to the gas chamber, or whether he had been murdered, I felt neither pity nor compassion for him. As a tool of the Germans, he refined and implemented their policies; he saw to the deportation of the infirm and the old, orphans and other children, and I could not be sorry that he perished.

*Rumkowski with children before the war*
*(Note Polish flag, Rumkowski's ill-fitting suit,*
*no stars on children's clothing)*

*Lodz, Poland*

## 7

## ❧ *The Arc of Transition* ❧

W E LOST TRACK OF TIME AS THE HOURS RAN INTO
seemingly endless days and nights. After what might have
been thirteen or fourteen days, we were ordered to line up
for "inspection," which entailed our running naked past a
team of three German officers. One of the Germans motioned us to either the right or left, and whispers ran
through the ranks that this was Mengele. I and others
were directed to the right and remained, awaiting we
knew not what, and those who had been directed to the
left were marched away. We soon lost sight of them, and
never again were they seen or heard of.

The ordeal of Auschwitz was over for us. The Germans threw us each a rag that looked like a coat and a
pair of shoes without regard to size, and loaded us into
cattle cars. Some fifty hours later, our transport came to a
halt, and we found ourselves at Arbeitslager Dessauer
Ufer. In a short time, I learned that we were at the outer
harbor of the city of Hamburg.

Dessauer Ufer turned out to be a slave labor camp,
and we were made to clear debris from bomb damage.
With our bare hands we moved bricks, rocks, glass, and
metal. It was some time in November of 1944, and we
were freezing. We did not have adequate clothing to wear,
we did not have enough to eat, and we were beaten.

After several weeks of this treatment, we were trans-
ported again; this time to Konzentrationslager Neuen-
gamme-Arbeitslager Sasel—another slave labor camp, on
the outskirts of Hamburg. Here we moved heavy concrete
squares and built temporary housing for the Germans
who had lost their homes in bombings by the Allies.
These houses, although both small and primitive, were
considerably more comfortable than the barracks to
which we were assigned. Once more, we worked like
beasts in the rain and bitter cold. It was now winter, and
well below zero; our clothes were threadbare, and we were
starved and had had no rest. We had been sapped of
strength and drained of hope. By January 1945, we asked
only one question of ourselves: *How long can we last?*

In March, we were once more on the move. The Germans ordered us to climb onto trucks, and we were dri-
ven toward Hannover—a distance of about two hours.
Once at our destination, we were ordered to walk. We
now began a long march on a dusty road that seemed to
be without end. When we finally came to an open gate
and marched through it, we were told we were in Bergen-
Belsen—the existence of which we knew nothing. More
than four hundred of us, women of all ages, were beaten
and pushed into barracks, smaller than the last, with but
a single, small window. Once inside, we were left to our
own devices. The latrines were far away, filthy, and unus-
able. The paths to them were strewn with dead, decaying
bodies, and a huge pit nearby contained thousands of
skeletons of the naked dead; the stench was unbearable—
but what were we to do? Food, if it reached us at all, came
after our first few days there, and we quickly began to
succumb to typhoid and dysentery. Those who had been
in Belsen for any length of time had become *Muselmän-*

*ner,* devoid of hope, and barely capable of standing on their feet. We looked upon the dead and dying, and resigned ourselves to the same fate. We could not last, and we did not have long to wait.

On April 15, 1945, Bergen-Belsen was "liberated" by the British army. We were now technically free and ironically unable to rejoice. We were still prisoners, and we were still interned, as the British were afraid of typhoid—which was rampant—and our anger at the Germans. As a result, they left us with two distinct impressions: that our care was not of paramount importance, and that we could not be trusted.

Our families and the life we knew were gone, and the road ahead was full of obstacles. In 1945 not one nation welcomed displaced persons or offered them asylum, but in six years the picture would change—largely because of the help of relatives abroad, the Jewish Refugee Committee, or friends.

Due to a unique set of circumstances, I was among the few who were fortunate enough to leave Germany in December 1945. Before my departure, I learned that Szaja was alive and had returned to Poland, and that Luba was in a displaced person's camp in the American sector of Southern Germany. The confusion of the times and the inexactitude of the data I received precluded my contacting or seeing them.

I had gotten a job working as a translator for the British army—which kept my mind busy—but the desire to leave Europe was never far from my thoughts. The chances of realizing my dream were of course slim, because I did not know anyone who could facilitate the process for me. In the summer of 1945, however, I handed over the names of forty former Sasel SS guards to the

British War Crimes Division; these men and women were apprehended and subsequently arrested. I was present at their pre-trial hearing, was called upon to testify, and a week later began to receive threats on my life. I was not safe even in a defeated Germany—and, in great haste, the British took the initiative to drive me to Paris, the only place in Europe that had an active American Embassy, and where I could hope to obtain a visa. Paris did not feel like a safe haven to me. When my uneasiness led me to look over my shoulder, I knew I had to leave Europe as soon as possible.

The Paris of 1945–46 was war torn, and conditions were poor. Food was rationed, bread was in short supply, housing was impossible to get, and heating fuel was non-existent. My sole comfort was the cot I slept in at the dormitory of the Jewish Youth Hostel at 4 bis rue des Rosiers. Although I was free, my life had not improved. I told myself, "This is only temporary," and tried to concentrate on obtaining a visa from the American Embassy or getting a certificate to Palestine through the British authorities. I was lost as never before, and lonelier than ever.

The Jewish men who had survived the war and come to Paris were housed on the fourth floor of the youth hostel, while we women were situated on the floor below. This propriety seemed very sweet to me after what we had been through. Since everyone was busy, the only greeting or friendly word I received in all the time I was there came from a tall, young man with watery blue eyes—a quiet man whose name was Julek. On occasion, the two of us went to a movie or had a glass of tea at Goldenberg's across the street. After a while one day over tea, I asked him to tell me where he came from and where he had been during the war.

Julek was surprised that I had taken any interest in
him, and it was heartbreaking to hear him say, "No one
has ever asked me about myself; no one has ever cared."
When he spoke, he blushed and stuttered. This is how he
began:

"I know that I was brought to the orphanage at Helenowek in Lodz at a very young age. My parents and sister
lived in a nearby village, and my father worked as a car-
penter. The family was embarrassed by my stammering
and came to the conclusion that I should be in the orphanage, but I hated the place and longed for my family
and our village. No one came to visit me; my childhood
was loveless and lonely, and I was trapped in an existence
bound by rules."

Startled to learn that he came from Lodz and that he
had been at Helenowek, I interrupted him to ask if he
knew Luba or Bronia. He smiled and said: "Yes, of course
I knew them. Where are they? Do you know?"

I shared what I knew, and Julek nodded. "I remember
that the three of us talked to a man named Sergei, just
before the outbreak of the war. It was the summer of 1939,
and he promised to help us."

I now clearly remembered what Shmuel had told me
about Sergei's efforts to help the children abused by Rumkowski, and felt I had to ask: "Did it have to do with the
molestations at the orphanage?"

Julek was taken aback. "Yes," he mused. "Rumkowski
molested the girls, and at times even the boys. I am sorry
to say that I was among them." He paused, and then
asked: "What happened to him?"

"As far as I know, he was killed in Auschwitz." How he
perished I could not say.

Julek began to reminisce: "When the Germans occupied Poland in '39 and appointed Rumkowski the 'Elder of the Jews'—and this was followed by the establishment of the ghetto six months later—I knew I would have to leave. I was afraid of Rumkowski as of no other man, because he was capable of anything. When word got around that Rumkowski planned to transfer the children to a new orphanage in the ghetto, and that it probably would be located in Marysin, the time to act had come. I gathered my few belongings, packed a knapsack, and left without saying a word to anyone.

"In the darkness before dawn, I took my knapsack, left Helenowek, and began to walk. When I was lucky, a friendly farmer gave me a ride on his wagon. I stole food, slept in fields and barns, and lived in fear of being caught by either the Germans or the Poles. After weeks of living like a vagabond, I ran across a band of young men. They were dirty and ragged, carried guns or pistols, and called themselves 'partisans.' Like me, they lived by their wits, stole food, hid by day, fled by night, and, on occasion, sabotaged a German train or killed one of the German guards. They were a bit older than I, but when they asked me to join them, I accepted. Since not one among them was a Jew, I claimed to be Catholic. We roamed the forests, always a step ahead of the Germans, and survived by scrounging around for food in the fields or, more rarely, on farms. Once in a while, a kind farmer gave us a loaf of bread, or we got hold of beer or vodka. The others got drunk; they became noisy and rambunctious, but I only pretended to drink. I was afraid of giving myself away."

Julek stopped. He rubbed the right side of his cheek and I waited, but he did not go on until I pleaded with him. First, however, he pointed to his face. "Can you see the indentations and scars on my cheeks?" I nodded that I could.

"One night in the woods, a comrade pulled the trigger of his revolver while in a drunken stupor. The bullet he discharged went astray, pierced the right side of my cheek, and came out on the left. I bled profusely, and my comrades wrapped rags over and around my head and cheeks. There were no doctors, hospitals, antibiotics, or painkillers available, and it took weeks before the wounds healed. All that remains are the fading scars and two indentations."

Julek sighed and continued:

"From '39 to '45, we roamed the forests, villages, and small towns, again always a step ahead of the Germans. We killed several Germans, derailed several trains, and blew up a truck or two. Almost five years of my life were spent in this way."

When he fell silent, I asked: "And when the war ended, and the Russians occupied Poland?"

"We disbanded. Most of the men returned to their homes, and I made my way to Lodz. I went to the village in which I was born."

I asked: "Did you find your family?"

"No. Everyone was gone. There was no longer any reason for me to stay, and I again set out on foot. I slowly made my way to Germany and, for a while, I lived in a DP Camp—but I couldn't stand it, so I began to walk and hitchhike until I arrived here. Like you, I am trying to get to the States. It is difficult, but I have hope."

In the months that followed, I never heard Julek speak of the past again.

Midway on my daily walk to the Metro along rue St. Antoine and toward place des Vosges I often sat on a bench in a little park bordered by fourteenth-century buildings. I loved this park because it was so peaceful there, and it became my sanctuary. As I continued my walk, I passed a small, dimly lit antique store with an almost-empty showcase in it. The owner, a short, dark-haired woman in her forties, invariably stood in the door-way, her haunted look seeming to beg for a customer. She always smiled at me, and I always smiled at her—but we did not speak. My appearance alone must have made it abundantly clear that I did not have the money to pur-chase antiques.

I found the shop window irresistable and, whenever the items in the showcase were changed, I stopped to admire the display. One day, I was particularly drawn to a small silver spice box adjacent to a silver picture frame. The intricate workmanship of the spice box so appealed to me that I decided to enter the shop and ask about it.

A heavy perfume hovered in the air—and behind the counter, smiling at me, stood the lady I had seen on so many of my walks. "How much is the silver spice box in the display case?" I asked, and the woman shook her head. "I am sorry; it is not for sale." Taking a breath, she explained: "I show it to be near to its beauty. When others admire it, it makes me happy. You see, it once belonged to my mother...May I show you the silver frame to the left?"

Before I could say a word, she removed the frame from the showcase and placed it in my hands. Within it was the faded photograph of an Eastern European family group. The women wore stiff, black dresses; the men, dark suits and skullcaps. It was clearly an intergenera-tional, traditional photo—the older men wore full, long beards, and the children sat in the front row—and yet it was very evocative. Over and over again my attention was captured by the image of a child—a little girl on the right, who looked about five. She wore a dark dress, long black stockings, and lace-up boots. There was a large bow in her hair, and her face was serious as she squinted at the camera. *What was it about her? Why did I have the eerie feeling that I knew her?* Without realizing what I had done, I gently ran my fingers across her face. In shock and as if struck by lightning, I blurted: "Little Bronia!"

The woman turned pale; she looked at me, and stammered: "How do you know? She is my cousin!"

"Where did she live?" I asked as calmly as I could. I needed an anchor—but when she said: "In Lodz," her words convinced me she and I were speaking of the same person.

When the woman asked how it came to be that I knew Bronia, I remembered every detail. "In 1942 I met her in the Lodz Ghetto. We worked in the same office," I responded. But she wanted to know what had happened to her and pressed me for details.

It took me a long time to reply. "She was deported from the ghetto in '44, but I don't know anything beyond that."

The woman had saddened. "I tried to locate my family! I searched, I inquired, I wrote! But nothing! Not a word from anyone! Still, I formed the impression that Bronia grew into a brilliant young woman! Was I right?"

I thought of Bronia, who conveyed messages from Rumkowski's office to ours. I thought of her brightness and her quick wit; her deformed body, wretched loneliness, and the tyranny of Rumkowski's abuse—and then, I nodded that she was indeed right. Bronia was precisely as she had perceived.

Gently removing the faded picture from its beautiful, ornate frame, the woman surprised me by saying, "I will keep the photo; you may have the frame."

I needed to know how much it was, but she said:

"This is my gift to you," as she wrapped it in tissue paper. When I protested, "Please let me pay," she shook her head emphatically. "You knew a part of my family, and I will not accept money from you." Her tone was very firm, and I could not argue. I thanked her, let her know that I expected to leave for America in a little while, and told her that I would see her again.

❦

In February of 1946, I received my visa and passage to the United States on the *Anson Mills*, a Merchant Marine ship sailing from Bordeaux and returning to the States with twelve passengers and no cargo ...

The day before I left Paris for Bordeaux, I went to the antique shop, as promised. The display case was empty and the door padlocked, but the sign above the door was still in place. Somewhat mystified, I went to see if the baker next door could explain the meaning of this. "The owner died a few days ago. She had no husband, no children, and in fact, no relatives at all. Someone came and took everything away. This is all I know," he replied. I thanked him, and left the bakery. For a long time afterward, I stood before the bolted door of the antique shop, with tears streaming down my face. I thought of the small, dark-haired lady, whose name I never knew, and little Bronia: two decent people I never again would see.

I bought a rail ticket to Bordeaux, got my seat assignment, and went to the hostel to pack. The next day, when I entered the compartment assigned to me on the train, I was struck dumb. Julek had bought the seat next to mine! "What on earth are you doing here?" I cried, and Julek smiled broadly: "I thought I would ride with you, and see you safely on board."

We were on a long, quiet journey through the night; the countryside was bleak and my thoughts dark as I remembered the cattle cars. By daybreak we were in Bordeaux, and we hailed a taxi to the harbor. Julek was in a quiet, reflective mood, and we barely exchanged two sentences between us.

At the gangplank I presented my documents and was allowed to board, but Julek had to plead for permission to accompany me. When he finally got it, it was on the condition that he leave within an hour. We deposited my things in the cabin I was to share with another woman, and went for a stroll. Julek, as it turned out, showed a keen interest in the canvas-covered life boats and the cargo hold—but details like these bored me, and I grew impatient. When the warning whistle sounded, guests had to leave, and we parted hastily. Before long, the boat edged away from shore to face the open sea. I looked for Julek, spotted him as he stood on the dock, and waved until he was no more than a dot on the horizon. At last, I could turn my eyes toward the vast sea.

Twenty-four days after I sailed from Bordeaux I arrived in New York. I was met by Lottie Strauss, a friend and former classmate, who brought me to her parents' home. For almost two agonizing weeks I was among people who saw me as a contaminated being from the camps, and I could not bear it. All the while, I faced an entirely new and frightening world. The city was awesome, and I was overwhelmed.

Lottie and her husband came to my rescue and helped me find a furnished room, as well as my first job in a glove factory. Because I hated the pressure of piecework and the low wages that were part of this system, I found a job as a secretary in an office. At home, the past: the war, my friends, parents, and sister, haunted my dreams—but when Rumkowski's angry face loomed before me, I awakened, screaming in fear.

Six months after I arrived, I received a telephone call from the Jewish Agency. Someone at the other end wanted to know if I was Cecilia Landau. When I said I was, the individual who called said: "One moment, please. I have someone here who wishes to speak to you." I waited, and to my great surprise, I heard: "Hello, Celia? This is Julek. I'm in New York. Where can we meet?"

After the moment it took me to regain my composure, Julek and I agreed to meet at six at the Sunnyside subway station. He did not speak English and he did not know the way, but the Jewish Agency would see to it that he understood how to get there. I decided to walk to the station, since it was not far from where I lived—but all the while, I wondered what Julek would have to say. As I walked, my thoughts were clear. I knew, for instance, that I did not want to become personally involved. I had met the man I was going to marry. Amazingly, I had known his parents in the ghetto—we had arrived on the same train but they were deported for "resettlement" in 1942 and vanished. Everyone close to us was now gone, and we wanted to hang onto the only remaining connection we had left to us.

I recognized Julek at once. (As he walked toward me, I noted that he wore a new gray suit, a white shirt with a dark tie, and brand new, black, wing-tip shoes.) We shook hands, and I greeted him warmly as a friend. "Welcome to America! When did you arrive, and what are your plans? Tell me at once!"

We fell into step, and Julek responded: "After you left, I felt I could not stay in Paris or anywhere in Europe. I had to get out." "But how did you manage?" I asked. I knew Julek had a story to tell, and I wanted to hear it.

"After I examined certain areas of the boat you were on, I decided to stow away on another Merchant Marine vessel—but it took me six months to gather the courage to do anything about it. For several weeks I spent a lot of time at the harbor in Bordeaux, hoping to learn about a sailing to America. When I finally did, I stole aboard with barely enough food and water to last the trip and hid in the cargo hold. Three of the longest weeks of my life were spent in cramped quarters and finally—*finally*, the boat docked in New York! I waited until nightfall before coming out of hiding, and in the morning I made my way to the Jewish Agency. I told them my story and they assured me of their help, but I will have to go to Canada first; after that, I can enter the States legally. Meanwhile, I have to learn how to speak English."

We chatted in this vein for a while—but our brief visit was winding down, and I regretted that I could not afford the twenty cents for a chocolate soda at the nearby drugstore. At the subway station, we again shook hands; I said: "I wish you the best of luck. I hope you will be happy, and that you will soon be able to enter the United States legally." These were common expressions, but I had meant every word. I knew only too well how much Julek deserved the chance to normalize his life.

Julek's last words to me were: "Will I see you again?" When I told him that I did not think so, and that I planned to marry, he turned away from me, entered the subway, and disappeared into the crowd.

*"Rumkowski" by H. Szylis*
*Lodz Ghetto, 1940*

8

# 8

## ⤙ *The Visit* ⤚

In the summer of 1975 I accompanied my friend, the poet Malka Heifetz Tussman, to Los Angeles. In our hotel room she introduced me to Sergei, a longtime friend of hers. This Sergei, as it turned out, was the same individual who had investigated the allegations of Rumkowski's molestation of children. I was in the presence of a man I had idealized, and about whom I had formed a mental picture that was both romantic and faintly idolatrous.

Not surprisingly, my image of a handsome, dashing figure did not match the actual physical reality and, at first sight, I was disappointed. Before me stood a man in his early seventies, about five feet, two inches tall, and stout—a man with a large, full face, double chin, light blue eyes weighted down by the huge, puffy bags below them, thick lips, enormous feet—from a certain point of view, the perfect anti-hero.

The real Sergei was understated, and seemed to be a kind, soft-spoken, gentle man—a person one could easily talk to—and we soon engaged in conversation. He told me he had been born, raised, and educated in Lodz, and he had escaped to Russia shortly after the Germans occupied Poland.

At a certain juncture, when I asked him if I could take

notes as he spoke, he agreed readily. I then began to cap-
ture the essence of our exchange, which went something
like this:

"I was born in Lodz in 1904, and lived there until
1939. By the early thirties I was active in the *Bund*, whose
members were secular Jewish socialists. During the same
time that I worked for the *Bund*, I also served as a councilman for the city administration. I had many friends
among both Jews and Catholics, but most of them remained in Poland after I fled. One of my friends is now a
well-known writer in Israel."

When I asked: "Are you speaking of Szaja Spiegel?" he
replied that he was, and when I offered to say: "I knew
him well during the three years we spent in the ghetto," he
wanted to know more about those years. I, however,
begged him to continue, promising to tell him whatever
he wished after he finished his story. Content to comply,
he went on:

"In 1939, just before the onset of the war, I filed a
complaint against Rumkowski with the Polish authorities. At that time, Rumkowski was working at the orphanage in Helenowek—where three children had lodged a
complaint against him. Weeping, they spoke of Rumkowski's 'indecent behavior'—but of course the war broke
out, and an official investigation did not take place."

I looked up from my notetaking. "Do you remember
a man by the name of Shmuel Berkowicz?"

"Yes, I do," he said, and then I described how I had
met him in the ghetto. "Once, we were friends," I added.
"He spoke about you and the children you tried to help."

Sergei, who had had no news of any of the principals,
wanted to know if I knew what had become of Shmuel
and the children—and I recounted the abysmal truth
of Shmuel's death by starvation; Bronia's deportation;

Julek's solitude, amazing strength, and resourcefulness; and Luba's life of misery, crushed innocence, and dreams. Since I left on the first transport signaling the liquidation of the ghetto and Rumkowski had left on the last, I could offer nothing new or precise about him.

When I was through, Sergei reached for my hand and said: "You have become my link to the past." Something intangible had touched us deeply.

Little by little, Sergei spoke of how he and his wife had fared on their flight from Lodz.

"Betty and I made it as far as a tiny village near the Polish-Russian frontier, where we stayed for a number of weeks. There, I met a young fellow willing to guide us through the woods and past various streams to the Russian side. We arrived at an agreement, but we knew there was always the possibility of betrayal—and I was afraid. One dark, cloudy night, however, he guided us across the border, and I paid him as I had promised. We shook hands, Betty and I rushed forward, and he headed home.

"Betty and I walked, rode on trains if we could, accepted help from peasants willing to give us a lift on a cart, and thus, slowly, made our way into Russia. I still had a little money and a few gold coins, but our existence was precarious—and I never stopped hoping that the war would end before our funds ran out.

"We fled through Russia and, since I spoke Russian, I was able to find work in the municipal offices of small towns. Once, I was appointed the commissar of a village. It was not what I wanted to do, but we had to survive; we had to eat, and I really had no choice in the matter.

"In 1943, the Russians accused me of being a spy. They imprisoned me, but, with the help of a fellow prisoner, I barely managed to escape. I was very lucky, because all this happened right before my 'trial.'

"Once again, Betty and I fled on foot. Sometimes, when the temperature fell to forty or more degrees below zero, we were given a lift on a horse-drawn cart. On the whole, however, we plodded on through high snowdrifts, just one step ahead of our pursuers. In Poland we were hunted by the Germans, and now we were being tracked by the Russians.

"I don't remember exactly how or when Betty and I got separated, but six months later we were reunited. By 1944, she and I had made our way to Japan; from there, we went to Canada, and from there to the States. We first went to Detroit, but eventually ended up in Los Angeles. I went back to school, and got a master's degree in social work—and that's it!"

Sergei stopped and sighed. He had been generous and open with information, and had not tired of answering my many questions. We had talked through the night—sometimes in English and sometimes in Yiddish—savoring even the smallest of details. All the while, Malka had listened quietly. She had heard Sergei's story before.

The following morning, after a quick breakfast, Sergei suggested, "I'd like you to go with me to visit Hela. She too was in the Lodz Ghetto and, like you, lived on Pawia 26."

I nodded my head, but at the moment only vaguely remembered her from the ghetto years. Hela, her husband, and their two small children, six and eight years old, had lived in the same building from 1940 to 1944 as had my mother, sister, and I. But beyond the casual hello, we barely spoke to one another, and never became friends.

I had not thought of Hela in years, but now Sergei spoke of her and awakened my memories.

"I am sure you have heard that her children were

taken during the ghetto *Sperre,* and with thousands of
other children were killed in nearby Chelmno. Her husband, Motek, died of starvation in the ghetto, and Hela
alone survived the war in Ravensbrueck."

"What became of her?" I wanted to know. Sergei did
not reply, but he picked up the telephone and made a call.

"Hela, this is Sergei. Celia, who used to live on Pawia
26 in 1942, is here right now. Can we come and visit?"
Sergei put the receiver down. "We can visit this morning,"
he said.

I was curious. "What happened to her after the end of
the war?"

"She came to the U.S. in 1953 and shortly thereafter
remarried. As a social worker I used to talk to her occasionally when she came to the Center. Her second husband, Moshe, was also from Lodz. I know she lived in the
Fairfax section of Los Angeles, and her second husband
died several years ago."

Sergei drove and I sat silently next to him. When we
reached our destination he parked the car, and after a
short walk we reached her apartment building. It was an
old neighborhood, and some of the buildings were badly
neglected.

"I want to warn you. Her second husband had a difficult and painful life, filled with unhappiness; but you'll
see ..."

We rang the bell. A small, white-haired woman answered the door. She greeted Sergei and shook hands with
me. She wore a plain, blue house dress and low-heeled
shoes, and had a sullen, pale face, devoid of all expression.
She did not speak. She just motioned for us to enter.

We followed her into what must have been the living
room, where my eyes had to adjust to the semi-darkness.

The drapes were drawn, and a single small table lamp gave an eerie glow to the room. The wallpaper was worn and dark green in color, the few furnishings old and shabby. We sat down. Hela still did not speak. She only looked at the faded photographs on the small table before her. I recognized her first husband and two small children. The photo must have been taken just before the war. The little girl smiled, and wore a large bow in her curly hair. The boy wore a suit, short pants, and a cap.

We continued to sit in silence until I finally burst out, "I remember Motek," and pointed to his photograph. Hela only nodded her head and repeated over and over again, "Murdered, murdered, all murdered," in a barely audible whisper.

I again tried to make conversation. "It is sunny outside. May we open the drapes?"

For the first time Hela looked straight at me and replied, "In all these years I have never opened the drapes. I just want to sit here and look at my children."

We were at a loss for words. There were no words to express her despair. The pain she felt for her murdered children would never leave her; her wounds would never heal.

Quietly we got up and took our leave. Hela paid us no heed.

✦

A year later I heard from Sergei that Hela had died as lonely as she had lived.

Sergei himself died in Los Angeles in 1988, but for many years after our first meeting, we visited one another and shared memories of Lodz and past events. Fortunate-ly, I was able to reconnect him with his boyhood friend, Szaja Spiegel. Their friendship rekindled, and sustained them the rest of their lives.

Luba survived Auschwitz as well as several work camps, and was liberated in 1945 in the American zone of occupied Germany. She spent the next three years in a displaced persons' camp. She looked for and eventually found Genek, but he rejected her brutally, discarding her like refuse. Eventually, she obtained a visa to the United States, where she married a man much older than she, and lived the life of a recluse. To the very end, she remained an unresolved, childless, angry, and bitter woman.

As for Julek, I never saw or heard from him again.

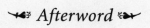 *Afterword*

THE ROLE OF THE ELDER OR CHAIRMAN WAS DIFFICULT and unenviable, particularly as it became clear that he had inherited a post that called upon him to weigh the fate of thousands on a daily basis. Could he preserve a delicate balance between life and death by acceding to German demands and turning over to them the young and the old, the weak and infirm? If the sacrifice were to be made, would productive workers assuredly survive? What were the alternatives? Was it to be: "Life for an hour is also life," or the Maimonedes injunction: "Better be all killed than one soul of Israel be surrendered"?

If such questions were considered to be unthinkable, how could they be acted on? Did one have a choice in the matter? In Brezeziny, Pabianice, Vilna, Warsaw, Kovno, and Lodz there were strong intimations as to the gassing of the children and the aged, as well as of the workers.[1] Reprisals for resistance were heavy, and yet the indomitable spirit took this route—and what is more, the Elders or Chairmen of the various Jewish councils were often at the forefront of these efforts. In Minsk, the Chairman, Eliyahu Myshkin, actively helped hundreds of young Jews escape to the forests—and yes, he was killed in an *action*, along with twelve thousand Jews. In Riga and in Kovno,

the Jewish police in the ghetto began to practice with fire-
arms by way of resistance, but in both instances they were
caught; in Warsaw, Janusz Korczak need not have accompanied the children in the Jewish orphanage over whom
he served as guardian—and yet, both he and the teachers
went with and took care of them, allaying their fears to
the very end. The children were never abandoned, and
everyone died together in Treblinka. Adam Czerniakow,
the head of the Council in Warsaw, committed suicide—
and why? In his diary entry of July 23, 1942, the very day
he took his life, he noted: "... They demand from me to
kill the children of my nation with my own hands ...
There is nothing left for me but to die...."[2] Rumkowski,
the Elder of Lodz, surely knew of this, as well as of other
accounts.[3]

The offering or forfeiture of oneself in the stead of
another, or as a demonstrable assertion against the un-
conscionable, is an aspect of human character that is both
well known and deserving of further research; certainly,
some of those enumerations may be made here—but that
is not, nor does it purport to be, our focus. If, however, we
chance to ask: "Was anything achieved by self-sacrifice?"
we would have to say that, like our great poets, each
teaches us how to live, what to do, and how to die.

From 1941 to 1943, when he was killed in Dachau,
Elchanan Elkes, head of the Jewish Council in Kovno,
faced the hard decisions with unblemished integrity, en-
couraging flight, resistance, and sabotage; not once was it
thinkable to turn over to the Germans a single Jew, and
not once did this happen.

In Chaim Rumkowski, we are not addressing such a
man. On one occasion, Rumkowski said: "... Dictatorship
is not a dirty word. Through dictatorship I earned the

Germans' respect for my work ... My ghetto is like a small kingdom.... For the price of fifty marks I got reports on all of the workers' top-secret meetings. In the meantime I set up a detention house, and slowly, one by one, I put the leaders inside..."[4] On another: "... And now I come to the plague known as gossip ... [A] gang of scoundrels is spreading rumors in the hope of disturbing the peace. Perhaps the authors of these panic-producing stories are lurking even here, in this audience. I would like to murder them!"[5] and still another: "... Children are always closest to my heart ...,"[6] however, in public Rumkowski stated: "... They are asking us to give up the best we possess—the children and the elderly. I was unworthy of having a child of my own, so I gave the best years of my life to children. I've lived and breathed with children. I never imagined I would be forced to deliver this sacrifice ... Brothers and sisters, hand them over to me! Fathers and mothers, give me your children...."[7] In these pages we learn, perhaps for the first time in print, just how, for all his "sincerity," the private Rumkowski measured up to his own words.

*Rebecca Camhi Fromer*

## NOTES

1. The children, sick, and elderly of Brezeziny and Pabianice were gassed in Chelmno, as reported by 1,420 survivors who entered the Lodz Ghetto on May 18, 1942; they estimated that 1,700 perished at that time. In addition, thousands of articles of clothing brought back into the ghetto for cleaning, repair, and redistribution to German centers were found to contain the distinctive currency of the Lodz Ghetto—the Rumkies—and other identifiable artifacts. Refer to Martin Gilbert, *The Holocaust* (New York: Holt, Rinehart & Winston, 1985), 348.

2. Gilbert, Martin, *The Holocaust* (New York: Holt, Rinehart & Winston, 1985), 387.

3. Since Rumkowski had access to and information from the Warsaw Ghetto, as did others (refer to Adelson and Lapides, *Lodz Ghetto* [New York: Viking, 1989], and the diary entry of Dawid Sierakowiak on July 27, 1942, page 270), this would constitute, at the very least, the second clearest indication of what would happen to the children consigned to the transports (see also note 1).

4. Adelson and Lapides, *Lodz Ghetto*, 146.

5. *Ibid.*, 199.

6. *Ibid.*, 232.

7. *Ibid.*, 328.

*A mural in Hamburg, Germany, in tribute to Lucille Eichengreen, incorporating her poem "Hair" with a photograph of her taken in Bergen-Belsen, October 1945*

THE ROOM IS FILLED WITH MOUNTAINS OF HAIR, BLOND, BROWN, AND BLACK, CURLY, WAVY, AND STRAIGHT. COLD BARE SCALPS—WHO HAD EVER HEARD OF WOMEN WITHOUT HAIR? THEIR SHINING STRANDS LEFT BEHIND. WHAT WILL THEY DO WITH THESE MOUNTAINS OF HAIR? "FILL PILLOWS, MATTRESSES, AND CHAIRS!" DOES IT BOTHER THOSE WHO USE THESE PILLOWS AND CHAIRS FILLED WITH HUMAN HAIR, DRENCHED WITH BLOOD, WITH TEARS, AND WITH CURSES?

## ❧ *Lucille Eichengreen* ☙

was born Cecilia Landau in Hamburg, Germany, in
1925. A survivor of the Lodz Ghetto and Auschwitz,
Neuengamme, and Bergen-Belsen concentration
camps, she fled to Paris in 1945 and then, in 1946,
made her way to New York, where she met her future
husband, Dan Eichengreen. In the following years,
she worked as an insurance agent while she finished
her education. In 1949, Eichengreen moved with her
husband to Berkeley, California, where their sons,
Barry and Martin, were born. Now retired, she writes
and speaks on the Holocaust at schools, colleges, and
universities. To find out more about Lucille Eichengreen and her first book, *From Ashes to Life: My
Memories of the Holocaust* (Mercury House, 1994),
please visit her website at www.webtran.com/lucille.

## ❧ *Rebecca Camhi Fromer* ❧

Peg Skorpinski

is the author of *The House by the Sea: A Portrait of the Holocaust in Greece* (Mercury House, 1999) and *The Holocaust Odyssey of Daniel Bennahmias, Sonderkommando* (The University of Alabama Press). She is cofounder, with her husband Seymour Fromer, of the Judah L. Magnes Memorial Museum in Berkeley, California. A teacher, poet, and playwright, she lives in Berkeley.